Letts

KS3

SUCCESS

CW00953352

MUCH ADO ABOUT NOTHING

Authors

Claire Crane & Juliet Walker

Published by Letts Educational
The Chiswick Centre
414 Chiswick High Road
London W4 5TF
Telephone: 020 8996 3333
Fax: 020 8742 8390
E-mail: mail@lettsed.co.uk
Website: www.letts-education.com

Letts Educational is part of the Granada Learning Group,
part of Granada plc.

First published 2005

ISBN 1 843153 831

British Library Cataloguing in Publication Data

A catalogue record for this book is available from the
British Library.

Commissioned by Cassandra Birmingham
Project management by Julia Swales
Editing by Vicky Butt
Cover by Starfish Design, London
Internal design by Ken Vail Graphic Design, Cambridge
Printed in Italy

CONTENTS

ABOUT THE PLAY

PLAY SUMMARIES & ANALYSIS

EXAM PRACTICE

PLOT SUMMARY

ACT 1

1. Don Pedro, Benedick, Claudio and company return victorious from the war and visit Leonato in Sicily.

2. Benedick and Beatrice, Leonato's niece, start squabbling and teasing each other as soon as they meet.

'a skirmish of wit'

3. Claudio falls in love with Hero, Leonato's daughter. Don Pedro offers to woo Hero on Claudio's behalf.

4. Jealous Don John, Don Pedro's illegitimate brother, plots against Claudio to ruin his marriage plans.

ACT 2

5. Don Pedro successfully woos Hero for Claudio at a masked dance.

6. Leonato, Don Pedro and others scheme to make Benedick and Beatrice fall in love with each other. Benedick hides in the orchard and overhears his friends discussing how much Beatrice loves him.

ACT 3

7. Beatrice hides in the orchard and overhears her friends discussing how much Benedick loves her.

8. Don John takes Claudio and Don Pedro to watch Hero apparently being unfaithful. They are really watching Hero's waiting woman, Margaret, with Borachio.

9. Conrade and Borachio discuss how their plot has succeeded. They are overheard and arrested by the Watch.

ACT 4

10. The wedding. Claudio refuses to marry Hero, saying she is dishonourable. Hero faints.

11. The Friar suggests everyone is told that Hero is dead. This will make Claudio realise what he is missing.

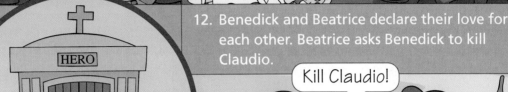

12. Benedick and Beatrice declare their love for each other. Beatrice asks Benedick to kill Claudio.

Kill Claudio!

13. Dogberry questions the prisoners and Don John's plot is explained. Don John has fled.

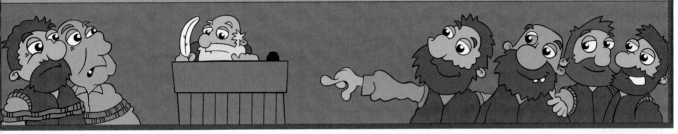

14. Now the full facts are known, Claudio offers to do anything to make up for his wrongs to Hero. He must marry a 'daughter' of Antonio – really Hero in disguise!

ACT 5

15. Hero unmasks herself. Benedick and Beatrice agree to marry and everyone is happy and united.

16. There is music and dancing before the marriages take place.

THE EXAM

DON'T WORRY!

A whole exam for 13-14 year olds on Shakespeare might sound a bit alarming to you at first, but you will be well prepared for it. You will know a great deal about *Much Ado About Nothing* before you go into the examination room - more than you could possibly write about in the time allowed. Your biggest challenge will be in selecting your best ideas to answer the question.

How long does it last?

Only 45 minutes.

When is the exam?

It will be in early May, in the same week as your other SATs papers. It will probably be on the same date as the English Writing exam.

How many questions should I answer?

Only one.

What do I take with me?

Just your writing equipment, including a highlighter (see page 75 to find out why).

If you are planning to take a number of items with you, then it is a good idea to buy a transparent pencil case. This is certainly the only sort of case allowed on desks in GCSE exams – so that you can't hide The Complete Works of Shakespeare in there!

In lessons your teacher may give you your own copy of the set scenes, which you can highlight and make notes on, or lend you a copy of the play. You must not take either of these into the exam with you.

What will it look like?

The question/task will be in an A4 booklet, which will also contain your set scenes (or extracts from them). You put your answer in a separate booklet. On the front you will find labelled spaces for your name and other school details.

How do I prepare for the exam?

It is important that you know what happens in the whole play, not just in your set scenes. The set scenes will make far more sense to you if you understand how the characters behave elsewhere.

Apart from reading the play, which you will probably do in class, it is also a good idea to watch it. After all, Shakespeare's plays were written to be watched by an audience – he had no idea that they would be read and studied by Year 9 pupils 400 years after they were written!

You can watch:

- A live performance. You may be lucky enough to find one at a local theatre. If so, your teacher will probably organise a visit.

- The film. There is a very good modern version, starring Kenneth Branagh and Denzel Washington.

THE TWO SELECTED SET SCENES

Each year the examiners choose two scenes for special study so that you can focus your attention closely on particular aspects of the play. Your teacher will tell you which scenes have been selected for your exam. The scenes might show different aspects of a character or a theme, so it is important to know what happens in the time between the scenes - you need to show that you fully understand what is going on. The exam question will refer to both scenes.

Make a chart like this to help you think about your scenes:

Act 1, Scene 1	Act 2, Scene 3
The opening scene, introducing most of the characters.	The sixth scene in the play, so we already know quite a lot about the characters. Benedick, Leonato, Don Pedro and Claudio feature.
We see Benedick in witty conversation with Beatrice and his male friends. He is confident and sociable and has opinions on all sorts of things.	Benedick is in hiding, eavesdropping on his friends. They are in control, because they have planned that he should overhear what they say. Benedick's speech is all made in asides – just heard by the audience.
Benedick is cynical about romantic love. He says he's not the marrying kind.	Benedick begins to change his attitude and is determined to be 'horribly in love' with Beatrice.
Benedick gives as good as he gets in conversations with Beatrice.	Beatrice has the upper hand, because Benedick is looking for a 'double meaning' in everything she says.
Benedick makes the jokes.	The joke is on Benedick, when he falls into his friends' trap.

What else could you add to this list?

THINGS TO THINK ABOUT WHEN READING YOUR SET SCENES

● At what point in the play do they take place?

● Which characters are in them?

● What do you learn about the featured characters?

● Does one character appear for the first or last time in either scene?

● Are any themes introduced or developed?

● Is there any interesting use of language?

● Are there any specific stage directions, such as music playing, asides, noises? What do these add to the mood of the scene?

SHAKESPEARE'S LANGUAGE

READING SHAKESPEARE

It is important not to be frightened off by Shakespeare's language just because it is a little different to our own. What might seem complicated at first sight can become far more straightforward if you remember to ...

● Use the glossary when reading the text. Remember, though, that it is not always necessary to understand every single word to grasp what is going on.

● Be guided by the punctuation. The meaning often runs on from one line to the next, even if it is set out like poetry. You will lose the sense if you stop after every line and do not read the whole sentence as one unit. Keep on to the next full stop!

DIFFERENT WRITING STYLES

Shakespeare has written much of this play in **PROSE**. You will be very familiar with prose because it is set out like normal text, not poetry. Most of the joking conversations, and ones between less noble characters, are carried out in prose.

In this play, Shakespeare sometimes switches between blank verse and prose without an obvious reason. The scene in which Benedick eavesdrops in the orchard is in prose, while the parallel scene with Beatrice is in blank verse.

When matters get very serious, for example when Claudio accuses Hero at the wedding, the dialogue is in **BLANK VERSE**. Shakespeare's blank verse has no rhyme, but there is a regular rhythm with ten syllables per line – a pattern called iambic pentameter. The text is set out to look like poetry, with a capital letter at the start of each line.

Writing styles in *Much Ado About Nothing*

Occasionally a pair of lines will rhyme, usually at the end of a speech or scene. These are called **RHYMING COUPLETS.** There are two rhyming couplets written in iambic pentameter in this play. See if you can spot them!

There are also some **SONGS** and **VERSES**. In Balthasar's song 'Sigh no more', every other line rhymes, while his one at Hero's tomb has short, rhyming couplets. Claudio reads out an epitaph in the form of a rhyming poem. Benedick attempts to write a **SONNET** for Beatrice – a formal, fourteen-line rhyming poem. He abandons the attempt because he has trouble thinking of suitable rhymes. As you can see, Shakespeare has provided a lot of variety in this play to add interest.

LANGUAGE

In Elizabethan theatres there were very few props and little scenery. There was certainly nothing high-tech in the way of lighting and sound effects such as those available to directors now. For this reason, a lot had to be spelled out for the audience through the language.

Shakespeare uses IMAGERY to create a clear picture for the audience and to contribute to the themes and atmosphere of his plays.

For example, in *Much Ado About Nothing* there is a lot of imagery involving fashion. Beatrice uses it to get across the idea that Benedick cannot be relied on to be constant in a relationship: 'He wears his faith but as the fashion of his hat; it ever changes with the next block.'

Sometimes a character uses a SIMILE to make their point vividly. This is when one thing is directly compared to another, introduced by the word 'like' or 'as'. For example, Benedick says that Beatrice exceeds Hero 'as much in beauty as the first of May doth the last of December'.

PUNS, or plays on words, appear frequently in the words of Beatrice and Benedick.

For example, when the Messenger says to Beatrice about Benedick: 'And a good soldier too, lady', she replies: 'And a good soldier to a lady.'

A METAPHOR is when one thing is described as being another, without the use of the words 'like' or 'as'.

For example, Leonato says that Hero has 'fallen / Into a pit of ink', which is an effective way of saying that her name has been blackened, or damaged, because of her dishonourable actions.

Language techniques

In ALLITERATION, the same consonant sounds are used, normally at the beginning of words, to create a particular effect.

For example, when Claudio accuses Hero he says, 'She's but the sign and semblance of her honour.' Notice that the 's' sound starts three words, and also ends two words. The whole effect is of Claudio spitting out his accusation in total disgust.

DOGBERRY'S LANGUAGE

Apart from the quick witted squabbling of Beatrice and Benedick, the most memorable language is the confused speech of Dogberry. About 200 years after Shakespeare wrote *Much Ado About Nothing*, a character called Mrs Malaprop was created by Sheridan in his play *The Rivals*. Mrs Malaprop has a way of using a word which sounds similar to the one intended, but has a totally different meaning, so the effect is humorous. The word 'malapropism' applies to some of Dogberry's misuse of language, such as using 'comprehend' (understand) rather than 'apprehend' (arrest). At other times he says the opposite of what he means, such as 'senseless' for 'sensible'. Sometimes he just uses entirely the wrong word, choosing one which has no link to what he really means. It is no wonder that Leonato loses patience with him.

Is our whole dissembly appeared?

SOCIAL, CULTURAL AND HISTORICAL BACKGROUND

THE STORY OF *MUCH ADO ABOUT NOTHING*

Shakespeare wrote many different types of play, including tragedies, comedies, histories and Greek and Roman plays. *Much Ado About Nothing*, written in 1598 or 1599 in London, is one of his comedies.

Shakespeare usually used older stories or poems as the basis for his work, but changed and developed the basic plots to make an original play. This was usual for authors of that time. For this play, Shakespeare has merged two storylines together. The Beatrice and Benedick one seems to be the more original. The Claudio and Hero plot, in which a woman is wrongly accused of being unfaithful, had appeared in a number of texts in the sixteenth century, but it cannot be known for certain which ones Shakespeare had read.

A COMEDY

Comedy in Shakespeare's time was not quite the same as that of the twenty-first century. Elizabethan audiences would have had certain expectations of the genre:

- Love would form the main theme, but there would be obstacles to overcome before the lovers could live happily ever after.

- The hero would be noble, but not without his faults, so the path of true love could not be allowed to run too smoothly for him.

- There would be confusion, often resulting from disguise or misunderstanding. Some plays would even have pairs of identical twins to add to the chaos.

- The characters would not be as fully developed as those in tragedies, many being stereotypes.

- There would, of course, be humour, often in the form of word play. This can be difficult for a modern reader at first, because some of the words have changed their meaning and some references are obscure.

- Most importantly, there would be at least one marriage – often more – at the end.

SETTING

Shakespeare set most of his comedies in foreign lands, very often in Italy. *Much Ado About Nothing* is set in Messina, on the island of Sicily off the coast of southern Italy.

Shakespeare had not travelled abroad, so made no attempt to set the scene realistically. Leonato's villa could just as well be an English country house, with its large gardens and orchard.

We know that some of the main characters are foreign to Sicily: Don Pedro is a prince of Arragon, a Spanish province; Benedick comes from Padua and Claudio from Florence, both cities in northern Italy. Florence had the reputation of being a place of culture and elegance, so Leonato would see Claudio as being a very good marriage prospect for Hero.

All the action takes place in or around Leonato's house and there is little sense of the outside world. A war is mentioned, but we are given no details of where this took place. It is possible that it was a rebellion set up by Don John against his brother, Don Pedro.

MARRIAGE IN ELIZABETHAN TIMES

In Elizabethan times, marriage was often regarded as an important business contract, not just as a union of two people in love. If your son or daughter married well, it could bring honour and respect to your family, and, of course, financial gain.

The question of honour and reputation is seen very clearly in the tragedy *Romeo and Juliet*, when Juliet refuses to marry Paris. In *Much Ado About Nothing*, Leonato at first thinks that Don Pedro might propose to his daughter. This would be a tremendous match for Hero. Leonato's extreme reaction when Hero is thought to be dishonourable shows how important a good marriage was. If Hero were guilty, not only would she have no chance of ever marrying, but the reputation and social standing of Leonato would suffer. In the case of Claudio and Hero it is clear that the couple are marrying for love, for no other motive is suggested when Claudio and Don Pedro discuss the marriage in Act 1.

THE STRUCTURE OF THE PLAY

Much Ado About Nothing is in five acts, as are all Shakespeare's plays. The plots of Elizabethan comedies were often complicated, with many twists and turns. They can be difficult to follow, but this play is largely straightforward.

For Shakespeare, Act 3 is usually the crucial one, containing a turning point in the story. This is true of *Much Ado About Nothing* because it is in this act that Don John's plot to discredit Hero works successfully. This only leaves two acts for matters to first go very wrong for the main characters, and then for everything to be resolved.

ELIZABETHAN THEATRE – VERY DIFFERENT TO NOWADAYS!

CHARACTER AND FUNCTION

In *Much Ado About Nothing*, we see characters from all layers of the small society of Messina. At the top is Don Pedro and at the bottom the Watch. There are a limited number of characters, with the storylines of marriage and Don John's wicked scheme closely linked.

In Shakespeare's comedies, the characters' names often give hints about their function and personality:

- 'Hero' would be a name well known to an Elizabethan audience because of the story of Hero and Leander from Greek mythology. Hero was entirely faithful to her lover, Leander, so the innocence of Shakespeare's Hero's and her devotion to Claudio would be taken for granted.

- Since Shakespeare was fond of puns, it is likely that 'Don John' was meant to suggest 'dungeon', which would fit with his criminal tendencies.

- Before the late 16th century, there were no proper theatres: plays were performed in noblemen's houses, outside inns, or in other open spaces.
- It was forbidden to perform plays in the city of London, because of the theatre's sleazy reputation.
- No women acted, which is why there are few women in Shakespeare's plays.
- Boys took the female roles.
- All performances were in the afternoon, because there was no stage lighting.
- When proper theatres were built, they were circular in shape – like the modern rebuilt Globe Theatre in London.

- The theatres could hold several thousand people.
- Part of the stage, and the area in front of it, was open to the sky.
- Plays appealed to all layers of society.
- You paid more money to sit in the covered area.
- You could stand at the front, as a 'groundling', and get wet if it rained!
- The stage was divided into three levels.
- There was no curtain.
- Actors had a lot of freedom in altering their scenes and dialogue.

THEMES

LOVE

Love is the main theme of *Much Ado About Nothing*. It is introduced in the first scene when Claudio returns from war and no longer looks at Hero 'with a soldier's eye' but falls in love with her. His thoughts and plans immediately turn to marriage, which would have been the natural course of events at the time.

Claudio and Hero are typical romantic lovers of the type seen in many comedies. They do not know each other very well, are attracted primarily by outward appearance, and the course of their relationship is guided by others. Shakespeare does not make the progress towards marriage easy for them, though, and it is not until Claudio realises the true value of Hero that he seen as being worthy of her.

The other pair of lovers, Beatrice and Benedick, provide a complete contrast to Claudio and Hero in their attitude to love and marriage, but they also need some outside intervention before their love can blossom. At first they both mock romantic love and cannot see themselves ever being married to anyone. They give the impression of being older than Claudio and Hero, because of their wider experience and views on relationships. Benedick is amused at Claudio's changed behaviour when he falls in love, including his new interest in music and fashion. When Benedick falls in love himself he tries at first to be a typical courtly lover, by writing a sonnet for Beatrice. He is not successful in his efforts and realises that he would get on much better by being himself. The way in which Beatrice and Benedick change, in order to allow themselves to fall in love, is to come to a better understanding of themselves – they drop their cynical attitudes, while retaining their good humour and wit.

APPEARANCE AND REALITY

The confusion between appearance and reality is a common theme in Shakespeare's plays, and in literature as a whole. In *Much Ado About Nothing* it is used for both comic and near tragic purposes. Much of the language and many of the ideas are linked to this theme – for example the imagery of clothing and the repetition of the word 'seeming'.

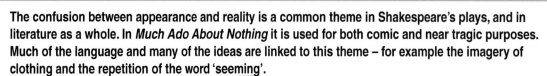

- Claudio falls in love with Hero largely because of her appearance. In this case appearance reflects the truth, for Hero is sweet and virtuous. However, when he later believes that she is dishonourable, he refers to her as a 'rotten orange' – in other words, looking good on the outside but mouldy inside. At the second wedding, Claudio must take the real appearance of his bride on trust.

- Don John gives the appearance of being loyal to his brother, however this is only to hide his devious plans.

- Benedick and Beatrice give the impression that they dislike each other, but this continuing 'skirmish of wit' just masks their true affection. Other people realise that they would be ideal partners before they do themselves.

- When Benedick and Beatrice hide to overhear their friends talking about them, they each hear a staged discussion, but do not suspect trickery. Benedick comments that if Leonato is involved, there can be nothing underhand – his age lends the scene the outward show of being genuine.

- There are real masks or disguises, both at the dance and when the ladies arrive for the second wedding ceremony.

- Dogberry's twisted use of language masks the true meaning of what he is trying to say. Yet despite this the criminals are caught and no lasting harm is done – things could have had a tragic outcome.

- The greatest example of being fooled by appearance is when Don Pedro and Claudio watch Borachio with Margaret and mistake her for Hero. This eventually teaches them that they must not judge by appearance alone, but should use what they know about a character, together with their own common sense, to arrive at the reality.

HONOUR

Honour was a code of behaviour strongly valued by Elizabethans. It is also important to the main characters in this play, all of whom are seen as honourable.

It is an honour for Leonato that Don Pedro should visit him. Even though the Prince has more status than Leonato, he shows him due honour and respect in his home. Hero's marriage to Claudio, a close companion of Don Pedro, would be a great honour, which would reflect well on Leonato's family.

When Don Pedro and Claudio think they have witnessed Hero being unfaithful, they denounce her publicly, because they feel that their honour and reputation have been marred by the attempt to marry Claudio to 'a common stale' (prostitute). They need to show that they are prepared to defend their honour.

In the same way, when Hero is proved to be innocent, Leonato demands that Claudio makes a full public acknowledgement of this. When he thinks his daughter is guilty, Leonato speaks heatedly about her 'shame' and sees death as better than living with this.

The characters' sense of their own honour and the respect due to them is reflected humorously in Dogberry's confused speech when he shows his self-importance and wants to be publicly acknowledged as an ass!

OTHER MOTIFS AND IMAGES TO WATCH OUT FOR ...

Food and eating

'Here's a dish I love not; I cannot endure my Lady Tongue.' (Benedick about Beatrice)

'His words are a very fantastical banquet, just so many strange dishes.' (Benedick about Claudio)

'Is it possible disdain should die while she hath such meet food to feed it as Signor Benedick?' (Beatrice)

Overhearing

Look out for anything to do with noting (a pun on the 'Nothing' of the play's title). This includes anything to do with eavesdropping, watching and writing. Here's one to start you off:

'I will show you enough; and when you have seen more and heard more, proceed accordingly.' (Don John to Don Pedro and Claudio)

Disease and medicine

'He will hang upon him like a disease.' (Beatrice about Benedick's friendship with Claudio)

'Any impediment will be medicinable to me.' (Don John about ruining Claudio's marriage)

War and fighting

'There is a kind of merry war between Signor Benedick and her; they never meet but there's a skirmish of wit between them.' (Leonato)

'Thy slander has gone through and through her heart.' (Leonato's accusation to Claudio)

Clothing and fashion

'He wears his faith but as the fashion of his hat; it ever changes with the new block.' (Beatrice about Benedick)

'Your grace is too costly to wear every day.' (Beatrice to Don Pedro)

CHARACTERS

ABOUT THE PLAY

HERO

'a modest young lady'

'the lady is very well worthy'

Hero is Leonato's daughter. She is a traditional Shakespearean character and she is shown to have the qualities which an audience in the 1600s would expect of a heroine. Don Pedro even refers to her as 'well worthy'.

She is shy, beautiful and modest, and unlike Beatrice she obeys her father's wishes and does not speak inappropriately. She is never asked about whether she wants to marry Claudio or even Don Pedro, she just agrees to whatever her father demands.

Her character is developed when she becomes involved in the Prince's plan to unite Beatrice and Benedick – a task she happily undertakes 'to help my cousin to a good husband'. Hero is a sensitive, but naïve young lady, yet she understands how important a good marriage is.

Her gentle nature is further developed when she listens to Claudio's unfair accusations about her supposed adultery. She does not shout or exclaim her innocence, but asks a few simple questions such as 'Is it not Hero?', before fainting from the shock and the injustice.

'the sweetest lady that ever I looked on'

At the end of the play, after revealing to a repentant Claudio that she is not dead, she seems happy to take him as her husband, even though he behaved very badly towards her. This might make her appear weak, but in fact she is only acting in the way that the audience would have expected.

'this rotten orange'

CLAUDIO

Claudio is a young soldier who fights in Don Pedro's army. He first sees Hero before the war, but when he returns he confirms he has fallen in love with her and agrees to let the Prince court her on his behalf. He is presented as a tempestuous, young and passionate gentleman.

He is concerned that he cannot woo Hero himself because he does not know the right words. Initially it seems that he has only fallen for Hero's looks and does not really love her, but Benedick reveals that he is heart-sick with love, reciting poetry and worrying about his appearance.

When he thinks that Hero has been unfaithful he is angry and jealous and does not stop to think about whether the rumours might be true. To a Shakespearean audience this would be proof of his affection and honour.

By the end of the play, he is sorry and even agrees to marry an unknown woman to show his repentance. His reward is to be reunited with Hero, whom he really loves.

'He has borne himself beyond the promise of his age, doing in the figure of a lamb the feats of a lion.'

'Count Comfect'

'a very forward March-chick'

'the right noble Claudio'

'Lord Lackbeard'

BEATRICE

'she were an excellent wife for Benedick'

'possessed with a fury'

Beatrice immediately strikes the audience as a lively, 'pleasant-spirited' young woman, with a sharp wit, who is not afraid of speaking at length and of saying what she thinks.

She provides a clear contrast to her reserved cousin Hero. She is close to Leonato, her guardian and uncle, and is fiercely loyal to Hero when she is dishonoured by Claudio. She supports Hero, when her father doubts her, and even instructs Benedick to kill Claudio.

She differs from the standard young woman of the time in her critical attitude to marriage and to romantic love, so she undergoes development during the play as she realises her true love for Benedick. This comes as little surprise to the audience, since she is obsessed with Benedick from her first words in Act 1. She constantly battles with him, being a good match for him in language and in love.

There might have been some relationship between them in the past, for she tells Don Pedro that Benedick lent her his heart for a while.

Whatever happened at that time, it is clear that neither can ignore the other and that, despite the harsh words, a strong fascination for each other still exists.

Beatrice has strong opinions and a proud, disdainful attitude, as her cousin points out, but she mellows when she realises this and throws herself wholeheartedly into being in love with Benedick.

'a pleasant-spirited lady'

'Lady Disdain'

BENEDICK

'Signor Mountanto'

'the Prince's jester'

Benedick is the main character of the play and offers a contrast to Claudio, the young romantic lover. He is discussed by other characters before he appears.

His wit, outgoing character and similarity in attitude to Beatrice are seen at once. He, too, is cynical about the idea of romantic love and does not see himself ever getting married. Like Beatrice, he is blinded to his true nature and feelings until they are cunningly pointed out to him in the orchard.

He is a valiant soldier and good friend to Don Pedro and Claudio. They in turn regard him as good value because, like Beatrice, he is always cheerful and entertaining – she refers to him as 'the Prince's jester', because Don Pedro seems to rely on him for humorous conversation. When Claudio dishonours Hero, Benedick has to reject his friends, whom he believes to be in the wrong, and support Beatrice and her cousin.

He very readily accepts that he is completely in love with Beatrice, despite his strong protestations about marriage beforehand, and is not ashamed about this turn-around. He realises that people do change their minds and behaviour and that is just one part of being human. He has a dominant role, and his words end the play.

'I will live a bachelor'

'He is of a noble strain, of approved valour, and confirmed honesty.'

LEONATO

Leonato, the Governor of Messina, is the father of Hero and uncle of Beatrice. All the action takes place in and around his property.

He is an old friend of Don Pedro, and shows his kindness and hospitality in having the Prince and all his companions to stay for a month.

He loves his daughter and is therefore delighted that she is to marry Claudio – a daughter well-married will also bring honour to his family. He is devastated when Hero is suspected of being false to Claudio and considers her death to be preferable to her living with dishonour. At first he believes that the accusation is true, rather than trusting his daughter. When he suspects that she is wrongly accused, he is aggressive towards Claudio and Don Pedro and behaves in an undignified way, but regains his dignity and courtesy when the full truth is known.

He shows his lighter side in joining the plan to make Benedick fall in love with Beatrice, and in enjoying the witty conversations between Beatrice and Benedick.

'the white-bearded fellow'

'my dear friend Leonato'

'good old man'

DON PEDRO

Don Pedro, Prince of Arragon, is the highest ranking character in the play. Despite his social status, he mixes easily and courteously with everyone. He is a man of noble qualities, who has gained victory in the recent war. He has forgiven his brother and has included him in this social visit to the home of Leonato.

He is quick to see the best in others, but can be too trusting and rely too much on outward appearances. This is why he fails to see that his brother is only reconciled to him on the surface, and why he accepts that Hero must be guilty without question. When he realises the truth, he is sincerely apologetic.

He is closely involved in both love stories. He is unselfish in helping Claudio to gain Hero, and he is keen to see his friend Benedick happily married. At the end of the play, when both marriages have been arranged, Don Pedro remains alone, with the problem of dealing with his villainous brother.

'Sweet Prince'

Prince, thou art sad; get thee a wife ...'

'Your grace is too costly to wear every day.'

ANTONIO, MARGARET AND URSULA

These characters all fulfil a function, but they are two-dimensional. Antonio is Leonato's brother and through their conversation we see the full extent of Leonato's distress after the shaming of Hero. Antonio supports his brother, is willing to fight Claudio and Don Pedro, and it is his 'daughter' that Claudio is meant to marry.

Margaret and Ursula are both attendants on Hero. They have a close relationship with the family and are involved in the plot to bring Beatrice and Benedick together. Margaret is the more memorable – she has a lively wit and it is her involvement with Borachio which, unknown to her, makes Don John's plot successful.

DON JOHN

Don John is an illegitimate son, which in Elizabethan times would mean that he was the villain of the play. Shakespeare's audiences would have believed that any illegitimate person automatically took on the sins of their parents in producing a child before getting married. This is a generalisation, but Don John openly admits that he is a 'plain-dealing villain' and conforms to the stereotype.

Although he has made peace with his brother, Don Pedro, Don John announces that he is an 'enemy of marriage' and will do anything to cause problems and pain to his brother or his brother's friends. He does not appear to have any positive qualities. He is moody and quiet and Beatrice exclaims that even his presence gives her indigestion. The mood of the play changes whenever he appears on stage and he does not hesitate to blacken Hero's name, even though she has done nothing to upset him personally. After causing 'mischief' he flees from Messina, but is caught, allowing the play to end happily. His close associates are Conrade and Borachio.

'I am not of many words'

w tartly that tleman looks.'

'I am a plain-dealing villain'

'He is composed and framed of treachery.'

'the devil'

'John the Bastard'

DOGBERRY, VERGES AND THE WATCH

Dogberry, Verges and the Watch provide the comic relief in a play which has many sad and upsetting moments. They are presented as foolish characters, although with dramatic irony they do comment on the actions of many of the main characters in the play.

Dogberry and Verges work for Leonato as officers, meant to keep the peace and patrol the streets. Shakespeare makes them talk in riddles sometimes, and muddles Dogberry's language in a way that an Elizabethan audience would have found very funny. Despite their foolish appearance, Dogberry and Verges are actually very important characters. Without them, Borachio and Conrade would not have been arrested and the truth about Hero's infidelity would not have been discovered.

'I am a wise fellow'

These characters are frustrating at times, especially when we need them to get directly to the point to relieve some of the tension but they refuse to do so. When Leonato demands that, rather than give their news Dogberry and Verges leave him in peace the night before his daughter's wedding, it builds tension for the audience – but we do understand how Leonato feels. Despite this, Dogberry and Verges are lovable characters and essential to the drama of the play.

'You have always been called a merciful man, partner.'

'Do not forget to specify ... that I am an ass.'

ACT 1

The action takes place in Messina in Sicily. The governor of the town, **LEONATO**, learns that **DON PEDRO**, Prince of Arragon, and a number of his friends and followers, will be arriving that evening after their victory in the war. This visit is an honour for Leonato.

A young man called **CLAUDIO** is reported to be highly valued by Don Pedro because of his brave fighting. Leonato's niece, **BEATRICE**, is eager to find out whether a soldier called **BENEDICK** has returned safely from the wars, though she speaks very critically of him.

Don Pedro arrives with his company and his illegitimate brother, **DON JOHN**, with whom he has only recently been on good terms. The soldiers are relaxed now that the war is over and plan to stay in Messina for a month.

Beatrice and Benedick immediately begin quarrelling and teasing each other. Meanwhile, Claudio's attention turns from war to love, as he notices **HERO**, Leonato's daughter. He had previously met her before the war, but now he confides to Benedick that he would like to marry her. Benedick makes it clear that he would never consider getting married himself. Don Pedro offers to woo Hero on Claudio's behalf at a masked dance that evening. Claudio agrees because it avoids the difficulty of proposing marriage to Hero, and because it would be awkward to refuse the suggestion of his high-ranking friend.

Meanwhile, Leonato talks to his brother **ANTONIO**. One of Antonio's servants has overheard Don Pedro saying that he is in love with Hero. Leonato is not sure whether this remarkable news can be true, but decides to prepare his daughter in case the Prince does propose to her. This is the first example of a misunderstanding in the play.

Don John, who is brooding and miserable, has also heard of the plan from his follower **BORACHIO**, but he hears the correct version. He is not pleased about the news because he resents Claudio, so plots to destroy his chance of happiness. He gains the agreement of **CONRADE** and Borachio to help him in a nasty scheme.

Line numbering

Other versions of the play that you read will probably have line numbers. Since Shakespeare did not leave a clearly set out, numbered manuscript of *Much Ado About Nothing*, different editions use different systems. We have decided to omit the numbers, because we did not want to cause confusion by giving different numbering to that used in your school text.

KEY TO THEMES

 love

 disguise/appearance versus reality

 nature

 gossip/overhearing

 food

 director's notes

 fighting

 marriage

 clothing

 honour

Act 1

Messina is a town in Sicily, an island off the coast of Italy.

The play begins with references to war and fighting. Many of Shakespeare's plays, especially the comedies, are about conflict and confusion that is solved by the end of the play. Fighting is one of the main themes of Much Ado About Nothing.

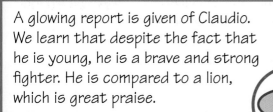

A glowing report is given of Claudio. We learn that despite the fact that he is young, he is a brave and strong fighter. He is compared to a lion, which is great praise.

Beatrice's very first line refers to the character of Benedick. She talks about him in negative terms, but it is important to notice that he is still the first thing on her mind when she hears that the soldiers are returning.

Like Claudio, Benedick is also praised for his good performance in the fighting.

none of name: no gentlemen
Florentine: people from Florence, in Northern Italy, were considered to be sophisticated, cultured and romantic
Signior Mountanto: a mountanto is an upward stroke in fencing; by using this name for Benedick, Beatrice is implying that he is 'stuck-up'
Cupid: the god of love
tax: criticise

SCENE 1. Before LEONATO's *house.*

Enter LEONATO, HERO *and* BEATRICE *with a* MESSENGER.

LEONATO: I learn in this letter that Don Pedro of Arragon comes this night to Messina.

MESSENGER: He is very near by this; he was not three leagues off when I left him.

LEONATO: How many gentlemen have you lost in this action?

MESSENGER: But few of any sort, and <u>none of name</u>.

LEONATO: A victory is twice itself when the achiever brings home full numbers. I find here that Don Pedro hath bestowed much honour on a young <u>Florentine</u> called Claudio.

MESSENGER: Much deserved on his part and equally remembered by Don Pedro. He hath borne himself beyond the promise of his age, doing, in the figure of a lamb, the feats of a lion; he hath, indeed, better bettered expectation than you must expect of me to tell you how.

LEONATO: He hath an uncle here in Messina will be very much glad of it.

MESSENGER: I have already delivered him letters, and there appears much joy in him; even so much that joy could not show itself modest enough without a badge of bitterness.

LEONATO: Did he break out into tears?

MESSENGER: In great measure.

LEONATO: A kind overflow of kindness. There are no faces truer than those that are so washed. How much better is it to weep at joy than to joy at weeping!

BEATRICE: I pray you, is <u>Signior Mountanto</u> returned from the wars or no?

MESSENGER: I know none of that name, lady; there was none such in the army of any sort.

LEONATO: What is he that you ask for, niece?

HERO: My cousin means Signior Benedick of Padua.

MESSENGER: O, he's returned, and as pleasant as ever he was.

BEATRICE: He set up his bills here in Messina and challenged <u>Cupid</u> at the flight; and my uncle's fool, reading the challenge, subscribed for Cupid, and challenged him at the bird-bolt. I pray you, how many hath he killed and eaten in these wars? But how many hath he killed? For indeed, I promised to eat all of his killing.

LEONATO: Faith, niece, you <u>tax</u> Signior Benedick too much; but he'll be meet with you, I doubt it not.

MESSENGER: He hath done good service, lady, in these wars.

This speech contains an extended metaphor about eating. Beatrice claims that Benedick only likes feasting.

Leonato explains that Beatrice (his niece) and Benedick have a battle of wits that is like a 'merry war'. Every time they meet they cannot help arguing and trying to outdo each other with jokes and clever language. The words 'war' and 'skirmish' are also connected to the theme of fighting.

Beatrice says that Benedick is not a good friend and is not very loyal. She claims that being friends with Benedick is like suffering from a disease. For someone who hates him as much as she claims, she spends virtually all her time talking about him! Do you think her feelings might run deeper than dislike, or might they even be the opposite? Either way, she certainly seems obsessed by him.

This is the first time that the young, male characters arrive. After everything we have heard about Benedick it will be interesting to see how he reacts to Beatrice and to see what she says to him face to face.

BEATRICE: You had <u>musty victual</u>, and he hath <u>holp</u> to eat it; he is a very <u>valiant trencher-man</u>; he hath an excellent stomach.

MESSENGER: And a good soldier too, lady.

BEATRICE: And a good soldier to a lady. But what is he to a lord?

MESSENGER: A lord to a lord, a man to a man; stuffed with all honourable virtues.

BEATRICE: It is so, indeed; he is no less than a stuffed man; but for the stuffing – well, we are all mortal.

LEONATO: You must not, sir, mistake my niece. There is a kind of merry war betwixt Signior Benedick and her, they never meet but there's a skirmish of wit between them.

BEATRICE: Alas! he gets nothing by that. In our last conflict four of his five wits went halting off, and now is the whole man governed with one; so that if he have wit enough to keep himself warm, let him bear it for a difference between himself and his horse; for it is all the wealth that he hath left, to be known a reasonable creature. Who is his companion now? He hath every month a new sworn brother.

MESSENGER: Is't possible?

BEATRICE: Very easily possible: he wears his faith but as the fashion of his hat; it ever changes with the next block.

MESSENGER: I see, lady, the gentleman is not in your books.

BEATRICE: No; an he were, I would burn my study. But, I pray you, who is his companion? Is there no young <u>squarer</u> now that will make a voyage with him to the devil?

MESSENGER: He is most in the company of the right noble Claudio.

BEATRICE: O Lord, he will hang upon him like a disease. He is sooner caught than the <u>pestilence</u>, and the taker runs presently mad. God help the noble Claudio! If he have caught the Benedick, it will cost him a thousand pound ere 'a be cured.

MESSENGER: I will hold friends with you, lady.

BEATRICE: Do, good friend.

LEONATO: You will never run mad, niece.

BEATRICE: No, not till a hot January.

MESSENGER: Don Pedro is approached.

Enter DON PEDRO, DON JOHN, CLAUDIO, BENEDICK and BALTHASAR.

DON PEDRO: Good Signior Leonato, you are come to meet your trouble? The fashion of the world is to avoid cost, and you encounter it.

LEONATO: Never came trouble to my house in the likeness of your Grace; for trouble being gone, comfort should remain; but when you depart from me, sorrow abides and happiness takes his leave.

<u>musty victual:</u> stale food

<u>holp:</u> helped

<u>valiant trencher-man:</u> someone with a good appetite; also implies good at fighting

<u>squarer:</u> boaster

<u>pestilence:</u> plague

DON PEDRO: You embrace your charge too willingly. I think this is your daughter.

LEONATO: Her mother hath many times told me so.

BENEDICK: Were you in doubt, sir, that you asked her?

LEONATO: Signior Benedick, no; for then were you a child.

DON PEDRO: You have it full, Benedick; we may guess by this what you are, being a man. Truly, the lady fathers herself. Be happy, lady, for you are like an honourable father.

BENEDICK: If Signior Leonato be her father, she would not have his head on her shoulders for all Messina, as like him as she is.

BEATRICE: I wonder that you will still be talking, Signior Benedick; nobody marks you.

BENEDICK: What, my dear Lady Disdain! Are you yet living?

BEATRICE: Is it possible disdain should die while she hath such meet food to feed it as Signior Benedick? Courtesy itself must convert to disdain, if you come in her presence.

BENEDICK: Then is courtesy a turncoat. But it is certain I am loved of all ladies, only you excepted; and I would I could find in my heart that I had not a hard heart, for, truly, I love none.

BEATRICE: A dear happiness to women; they would else have been troubled with a pernicious suitor. I thank God, and my cold blood, I am of your humour for that: I had rather hear my dog bark at a crow than a man swear he loves me.

BENEDICK: God keep your ladyship still in that mind! So some gentleman or other shall 'scape a predestinate scratched face.

BEATRICE: Scratching could not make it worse, an 'twere such a face as yours were.

BENEDICK: Well, you are a rare parrot-teacher.

BEATRICE: A bird of my tongue is better than a beast of yours.

BENEDICK: I would my horse had the speed of your tongue, and so good a continuer. But keep your way, a' God's name; I have done.

BEATRICE: You always end with a jade's trick: I know you of old.

DON PEDRO: That is the sum of all, Leonato. Signior Claudio and Signior Benedick, my dear friend Leonato hath invited you all. I tell him we shall stay here at the least a month, and he heartily prays some occasion may detain us longer. I dare swear he is no hypocrite, but prays from his heart.

LEONATO: If you swear, my lord, you shall not be forsworn. (To DON JOHN) Let me bid you welcome, my lord – being reconciled to the prince your brother, I owe you all duty.

Although a joke is made of it here, being born of wedded parents was very important. You can see this in the negative way that the bastard, Don John, is presented. Look at his speeches in Act 1 Scene 3.

This line is important. Beatrice makes a cutting remark to suggest that no one is listening to Benedick even though he keeps on talking. This has more significance later in the play when characters refuse to listen to others.

Benedick replies by calling Beatrice 'Lady Disdain' and remarking that he is surprised she is still alive. This is his way of joking that he does not care whether she is alive or dead.

These two characters now both claim that they do not ever want to be married. Benedick claims that he is loved by all women (except Beatrice) and yet has never found anyone to love. Beatrice says she would rather listen to a yapping dog than hear a man tell her he is in love with her.

This joking between the two characters would be powerful on stage as they both try to outdo each other. The pace of their lines should be quick, to demonstrate their quick-thinking and speedy comebacks.

Lady Disdain: 'disdain' means despising; Beatrice used a similar form of insult earlier ('Signor Mountanto')
turncoat: someone who turns against their own principles
pernicious: wicked
predestinate: unavoidable
parrot-teacher: mimic
jade's trick: a jade is a useless horse, Benedick is backing out of the contest like an old nag

Don John stands out because of his silence and aloofness. The fact that he says little contrasts strongly with Beatrice and Benedick, who do not stop talking.

Claudio draws Benedick's attention to Hero, commenting on her modest and shy qualities. Benedick is not impressed by her (probably because he is already in love with Beatrice, even though he would not admit it).

Claudio seems very much in love with Hero, but it is important that these lines are all about what a person sees. Claudio has fallen in love with her looks, not necessarily with her personality. Claudio admits to Benedick that he wants to marry Hero.

The theme of secrecy is introduced here. Don Pedro asks what the two men have been gossiping about. There are lots of occasions in this play where characters spread lies, swap stories and confide in each other.

Benedick tells Don Pedro that Claudio is in love with Hero.

flouting Jack: mocking rascal
Vulcan: the God of blacksmiths
allegiance: loyalty

DON JOHN: I thank you; I am not of many words, but I thank you.

LEONATO: Please it your grace lead on?

DON PEDRO: Your hand, Leonato; we will go together.

Exeunt all except BENEDICK and CLAUDIO.

CLAUDIO: Benedick, didst thou note the daughter of Signior Leonato?

BENEDICK: I noted her not, but I looked on her.

CLAUDIO: Is she not a modest young lady?

BENEDICK: Do you question me as an honest man should do, for my simple true judgment; or would you have me speak after my custom, as being a professed tyrant to their sex?

CLAUDIO: No, I pray thee speak in sober judgment.

BENEDICK: Why, i' faith, methinks she's too low for a high praise, too brown for a fair praise and too little for a great praise; only this commendation I can afford her, that were she other than she is, she were unhandsome; and being no other but as she is, I do not like her.

CLAUDIO: Thou thinkest I am in sport; I pray thee tell me truly how thou likest her.

BENEDICK: Would you buy her, that you inquire after her?

CLAUDIO: Can the world buy such a jewel?

BENEDICK: Yea, and a case to put it into. But speak you this with a sad brow? Or do you play the **flouting Jack**, to tell us Cupid is a good hare-finder and **Vulcan** a rare carpenter? Come, in what key shall a man take you, to go in the song?

CLAUDIO: In mine eye she is the sweetest lady that ever I looked on.

BENEDICK: I can see yet without spectacles and I see no such matter; there's her cousin, an she were not possessed with a fury, exceeds her as much in beauty as the first of May doth the last of December. But I hope you have no intent to turn husband, have you?

CLAUDIO: I would scarce trust myself, though I had sworn the contrary, if Hero would be my wife.

BENEDICK: Is't come to this? In faith, hath not the world one man but he will wear his cap with suspicion? Shall I never see a bachelor of threescore again? Go to, i' faith; an thou wilt needs thrust thy neck into a yoke, wear the print of it and sigh away Sundays. Look, Don Pedro is returned to seek you.

Re-enter DON PEDRO.

DON PEDRO: What secret hath held you here, that you followed not to Leonato's?

BENEDICK: I would your Grace would constrain me to tell.

DON PEDRO: I charge thee on thy **allegiance**.

BENEDICK: You hear, Count Claudio; I can be secret as a dumb man, I would have you think so; but, on my allegiance, mark you this, on my allegiance – he is in love. With who? Now that is your grace's part. Mark how short his answer is: with Hero, Leonato's short daughter.

CLAUDIO: If this were so, so were it uttered.

BENEDICK: Like the old tale, my lord: 'It is not so, nor 'twas not so, but, indeed, God forbid it should be so.'

CLAUDIO: If my passion change not shortly, God forbid it should be otherwise.

DON PEDRO: Amen, if you love her; for the lady is very well worthy.

CLAUDIO: You speak this to fetch me in, my lord.

DON PEDRO: By my troth, I speak my thought.

CLAUDIO: And, in faith, my lord, I spoke mine.

BENEDICK: And, by my two faiths and <u>troths</u>, my lord, I spoke mine.

CLAUDIO: That I love her, I feel.

DON PEDRO: That she is worthy, I know.

BENEDICK: That I neither feel how she should be loved, nor know how she should be worthy, is the opinion that fire cannot melt out of me; I will die in it at the stake.

DON PEDRO: Thou wast ever an obstinate <u>heretic</u> in the despite of beauty.

CLAUDIO: And never could maintain his part but in the force of his will.

BENEDICK: That a woman conceived me, I thank her; that she brought me up, I likewise give her most humble thanks; but that I will have a <u>recheat winded</u> in my forehead, or hang my bugle in an invisible <u>baldrick</u>, all women shall pardon me. Because I will not do them the wrong to mistrust any, I will do myself the right to trust none; and the fine is, for the which I may go the finer, I will live a bachelor.

DON PEDRO: I shall see thee, ere I die, look pale with love.

BENEDICK: With anger, with sickness, or with hunger, my lord, not with love. Prove that ever I lose more blood with love than I will get again with drinking, pick out mine eyes with a ballad-maker's pen and hang me up at the door of a brothel-house for the sign of blind Cupid.

DON PEDRO: Well, if ever thou dost fall from this faith, thou wilt prove a notable argument.

BENEDICK: If I do, hang me in a bottle like a cat and shoot at me; and he that hits me, let him be clapped on the shoulder, and called <u>Adam</u>.

DON PEDRO: Well, as time shall try: 'In time the savage bull doth bear the yoke.'

BENEDICK: The savage bull may; but if ever the sensible Benedick bear it, <u>pluck off the bull's horns</u> and set them in my forehead: and let me be vilely painted; and in such great letters as they write 'Here is good horse to hire', let them signify under my sign 'Here you may see Benedick the married man.'

CLAUDIO: If this should ever happen, thou wouldst be horn-mad.

DON PEDRO: Nay, if Cupid have not spent all his quiver in Venice, thou wilt quake for this shortly.

Love and marriage are important ideas in this play. All of Shakespeare's comedies involve people falling in love and eventually getting happily married. You should look for evidence of different kinds of love in the play. The way that Beatrice and Benedick feel about each other, for example, is very different from the way that Claudio feels about Hero.

Again Benedick claims that he never wants to get married and is very happy to live as a bachelor. Like Beatrice, do you think he is making too much of this? Would he secretly love to find a woman who could interest him and match his intelligence and humour?

Don Pedro wisely and ironically says that if Benedick does ever fall in love it will be quite a story. Benedick then seriously tempts fate by saying that if he does, he ought to be shot and hanged!

Benedick compares marriage to a form of slavery, saying that being a husband would be like being a beast of burden and working in the fields all day. He says that if he were to be a husband, his friends might as well attach two bull's horns to his forehead.

<u>troths</u>: allegiances/loyalty

<u>heretic</u>: person with controversial opinions and beliefs (usually religious)

<u>recheat winded</u>: a call blown on a horn

<u>baldrick</u>: a strap worn over the shoulders to support a sword or horn

<u>Adam</u>: Adam Bell, an outlaw mentioned in ballads

<u>pluck off the bull's horns</u>: bulls horns on a man's forehead were a symbol that he had been 'cuckolded', i.e. that his wife had been unfaithful

Don Pedro wants to accept Leonato's invitation to dinner, knowing how much effort has gone into preparing for him and his companions. He sends Benedick as a messenger. This is a way of getting Benedick off stage so that Don Pedro can discuss Hero privately with Claudio.

Claudio confesses to Don Pedro how he feels about Hero. He explains that he fell in love when her first saw her, but at that time his mind was taken up by his duties as a soldier.

This speech is important and Shakespeare draws our attention to it by having Claudio speak in BLANK VERSE. This form is often used for key speeches in the play, especially those featuring serious issues. Most of the other speeches in *Much Ado About Nothing* are in prose.

Look at how the themes of love and war are interwoven here.

Don Pedro offers to tell Hero and her father how Claudio feels as he is so nervous. Asking a friend to relay your feelings to the object of your desire would have been a fairly common practice in Tudor times.

Claudio is concerned about the speed of the arrangement. He thinks a longer build-up to the proposal might be seen as more appropriate.

temporize: act evasively to gain time
repair: go
affect: aim for
break with: discuss the marriage proposal
salved it: made it better

24

BENEDICK: I look for an earthquake too, then.
DON PEDRO: Well, you will **temporize** with the hours. In the meantime, good Signior Benedick, **repair** to Leonato's, commend me to him and tell him I will not fail him at supper; for indeed he hath made great preparation.
BENEDICK: I have almost matter enough in me for such an embassage; and so I commit you –
CLAUDIO: To the tuition of God. From my house, if I had it –
DON PEDRO: The sixth of July. Your loving friend, Benedick.
BENEDICK: Nay, mock not, mock not. The body of your discourse is sometime guarded with fragments, and the guards are but slightly basted on neither. Ere you flout old ends any further, examine your conscience; and so I leave you.
Exit.
CLAUDIO: My liege, your highness now may do me good.
DON PEDRO: My love is thine to teach: teach it but how,
And thou shalt see how apt it is to learn
Any hard lesson that may do thee good.
CLAUDIO: Hath Leonato any son, my lord?
DON PEDRO: No child but Hero; she's his only heir.
Dost thou **affect** her, Claudio?
CLAUDIO: O, my lord,
When you went onward on this ended action,
I look'd upon her with a soldier's eye,
That liked, but had a rougher task in hand
Than to drive liking to the name of love;
But now I am return'd and that war-thoughts
Have left their places vacant, in their rooms
Come thronging soft and delicate desires,
All prompting me how fair young Hero is,
Saying, I liked her ere I went to wars.
DON PEDRO: Thou wilt be like a lover presently
And tire the hearer with a book of words.
If thou dost love fair Hero, cherish it,
And I will **break with** her and with her father,
And thou shalt have her. Was't not to this end
That thou began'st to twist so fine a story?
CLAUDIO: How sweetly you do minister to love,
That know love's grief by his complexion!
But lest my liking might too sudden seem,
I would have **salved it** with a longer treatise.
DON PEDRO: What need the bridge much broader than the flood?
The fairest grant is the necessity.
Look, what will serve is fit. 'Tis once, thou lovest,
And I will fit thee with the remedy.
I know we shall have revelling to-night;
I will assume thy part in some disguise

And tell fair Hero I am Claudio,
And in her bosom I'll unclasp my heart
And take her hearing prisoner with the force
And strong encounter of my amorous tale.
Then, after, to her father will I break;
And the conclusion is, she shall be thine.
In practise let us put it presently.
Exeunt.

SCENE 3. LEONATO's house.

Don Pedro reassures Claudio and has a plan to smooth the romance along. During the masked ball, Don Pedro plans to disguise himself as Claudio. He will woo Hero, impressing her with his romantic words, then will tell her father that Claudio wants to marry her.

As the audience, you might already be able to see how this could be a dangerous situation, causing confusion.

SCENE 2 takes place in a room in Leonato's house. Leonato and his older brother Antonio are discussing Hero. Antonio believes that he overheard Don Pedro planning to ask for Hero's hand in marriage. The two men get very excited at this prospect, which would mean great honour to their house and they prepare to warn Hero.

Enter DON JOHN and CONRADE.
CONRADE: What the good-year, my lord! Why are you thus out of measure sad?
DON JOHN: There is no measure in the occasion that breeds; therefore the sadness is without limit.
CONRADE: You should hear reason.
DON JOHN: And when I have heard it, what blessing brings it?
CONRADE: If not a present remedy, at least a patient sufferance.
DON JOHN: I wonder that thou, being, as thou sayest thou art, born under Saturn, goest about to apply a moral medicine to a mortifying mischief. I cannot hide what I am. I must be sad when I have cause, and smile at no man's jests; eat when I have stomach, and wait for no man's leisure; sleep when I am drowsy, and tend on no man's business; laugh when I am merry, and claw no man in his humour.
CONRADE: Yea, but you must not make the full show of this till you may do it without controlment. You have of late stood out against your brother, and he hath ta'en you newly into his grace; where it is impossible you should take true root but by the fair weather that you make yourself; it is needful that you frame the season for your own harvest.
DON JOHN: I had rather be a canker in a hedge than a rose in his grace, and it better fits my blood to be disdained of all than to fashion a carriage to rob love from any. In this, though I cannot be said to be a

Don John discusses his own miserable and sad nature. He says that he cannot pretend to be something that he is not, just as when he is hungry he must eat something.

Conrade points out that Don John has recently been at odds with his half brother, Don Pedro. Although the brothers have been reconciled, Don John needs to behave himself if he is to stay in favour.

Don John says that he would rather be a wild rose (a canker) than a cultivated one. He might be suggesting that he is happy being illegitimate.

Don John admits freely that he hates everyone and is a villainous character through and through – he says it is in his blood. He says that at the moment he is forced to remain quiet, but soon he will have a chance to show his wicked side.

Don John's openness about his evil character is shocking, and creates tension for the audience. Although they are witnesses to his evil plans, they are only watching events and so are powerless to stop them. This is an example of how dramatic irony is produced.

Continuing the theme of eavesdropping, Borachio has overheard Don Pedro's arrangement with Claudio. Don John is delighted. He plans to use this news as a means to ruin the happy celebrations and cause his brother and Claudio upset.

flattering honest man, it must not be denied but I am a plain-dealing villain. I am trusted with a muzzle and enfranchised with a clog; therefore I have decreed not to sing in my cage. If I had my mouth, I would bite; if I had my liberty, I would do my liking. In the meantime, let me be that I am, and seek not to alter me.

CONRADE: Can you make no use of your discontent?

DON JOHN: I make all use of it, for I use it only. Who comes here?

Enter BORACHIO.

What news, Borachio?

BORACHIO: I came yonder from a great supper. The Prince, your brother, is royally entertained by Leonato; and I can give you intelligence of an intended marriage.

DON JOHN: Will it serve for any model to build mischief on? What is he for a fool that betroths himself to unquietness?

BORACHIO: Marry, it is your brother's right hand.

DON JOHN: Who? The most exquisite Claudio?

BORACHIO: Even he.

DON JOHN: A proper squire! And who, and who? Which way looks he?

BORACHIO: Marry, on Hero, the daughter and heir of Leonato.

DON JOHN: A very forward **March-chick**! How came you to this?

BORACHIO: Being entertained for a perfumer, as I was smoking a musty room, comes me the Prince and Claudio, hand in hand in sad conference. **I whipt me behind the arras**, and there heard it agreed upon that the Prince should woo Hero for himself, and, having obtained her, give her to Count Claudio.

DON JOHN: Come, come, let us thither; this may prove food to my displeasure. That young start-up hath all the glory of my overthrow. If I can cross him any way, I bless myself every way. You are both sure, and will assist me?

CONRADE: To the death, my lord.

DON JOHN: Let us to the great supper; their cheer is the greater that I am subdued. Would the cook were of my mind! Shall we go prove what's to be done?

BORACHIO: We'll wait upon your lordship.

Exeunt.

March-chick: a young upstart
I whipt me behind the arras: I hid behind a hanging tapestry

Understanding the plot
1. Who comes to stay with Leonato, Governor of Messina?
2. What reason does Leonato give for making Don John welcome?
3. Who does Claudio first tell of his love for Hero?
4. How will Hero learn of Claudio's love for her?
5. Who will help Don John in his scheme against Claudio?

Who says this?
1. 'I pray you, is Signor Mountanto returned from the wars or no?'
2. 'What, my dear Lady Disdain! Are you yet living?'
3. 'I am not of many words.'
4. 'I shall see thee, ere I die, look pale with love.'
5. 'In mine eye she is the sweetest lady that ever I looked on.'

Name the character
1. Who falls in love with Leonato's daughter?
2. Who has an uneasy relationship with his noble brother?
3. Who tells his brother of a rumour about Don Pedro wanting to marry Hero?
4. Who says that he will never get married?
5. Who overhears Don Pedro talking to Claudio and tells Don John what was said?

Understanding character
1. Who does Beatrice seem obsessed with from the start of the play?
2. Why has Don Pedro honoured Claudio?
3. Which of the men is a constant joker?
4. Why does Claudio agree to Don Pedro wooing Hero for him?
5. Why is Don John so jealous of Claudio?

Themes and imagery
1. Appearance/reality: Who appears to be loyal, when this is not really the case?
2. Love: Which characters are typical romantic lovers?
3. Fighting: Which characters take part in battles of wit?
4. Whose friendship for Claudio is described as if it were a disease, difficult to shake off?
5. Who is described insultingly as 'a very forward March-chick'?

ACT 2 SUMMARY

ACT 2

In the governor's house, Leonato, Antonio, Hero and Beatrice are having a discussion. Beatrice comments that Don John makes her feel uncomfortable because he never says anything. She makes everyone laugh and lists all the types of men she could never bear to marry. Leonato reminds Hero that she must answer 'yes' if the Prince asks her to marry him that evening.

Later, all the characters enter the hall in masks for a huge party. Don Pedro, performing his role as Claudio, dances with Hero and begins to court her. Behind their mask-disguises even Beatrice and Benedick begin to flirt together (although Beatrice refers to Benedick as a court jester, which upsets him). After most of the characters have left the stage, Don John and Borachio ask the disguised Claudio if he is Benedick. Claudio pretends that he is, and is shocked when Don John and Borachio tell him that Don Pedro has wooed Hero for himself. Claudio is furious because he thinks that Don Pedro has betrayed him and he leaves the party.

Claudio, Beatrice, Hero and Leonato come to speak with Don Pedro. Beatrice tells him that Claudio is jealous. Don Pedro explains the mistake and tells everyone that Hero

has agreed to marry Claudio. Hero and Claudio kiss. Don Pedro decides that Beatrice and Benedick would make a perfect couple and plans to get the two together. Everyone else agrees to help.

Don John is so annoyed by Claudio's proposed marriage that he decides to make trouble. Borachio has a plan. He will embrace Hero's servant **MARGARET**, in front of Don John, Don Pedro and Claudio. In the dusk and through the bedroom window, they will assume Hero is being unfaithful and the wedding will be called off.

Benedick enters the orchard complaining about marriage. He hides when he sees his friends and listens as Don Pedro, Claudio and Leonato begin to discuss Beatrice's love for Benedick. He learns that Beatrice would rather die than tell him how she feels. Benedick is left alone thinking about what he has heard, and suddenly realises that Beatrice is his perfect woman. When she calls him for dinner, he analyses every word she says and convinces himself he can see evidence of her love.

KEY TO THEMES

 love

disguise/appearance versus reality

nature

 gossip/overhearing

 food

director's notes

 fighting

 marriage

 clothing

 honour

Act 2

Beatrice believes that the perfect man would be a mixture of Don John, who says very little, and Benedick, who can't stop talking.

Leonato warns Beatrice that if she carries on being so sarcastic she will never find herself a husband. At this time, women were expected to be polite, quiet and shy – exactly like Hero, in fact.

Beatrice claims that she does not want a husband who is too old, nor one who is too young. Essentially, she does not want a husband at all. This attitude from a woman would be very unusual in Elizabethan times.

The idea of disguise is very important in this play and is referred to again and again.

Beatrice agrees that Hero is a more traditional female, who fits the ideal picture of a woman. This links to Claudio's first comment about her, that she is 'modest'. At this point she seems to be the opposite to the straight-talking Beatrice.

heart-burned: having indigestion
curst: bad-tempered
lie in the woollen: sleep between rough blankets
cuckold: a person whose husband or wife has been unfaithful

SCENE 1. *A hall in LEONATO's house.*

Enter LEONATO, ANTONIO, HERO, BEATRICE and others.

LEONATO: Was not Count John here at supper?

ANTONIO: I saw him not.

BEATRICE: How tartly that gentleman looks! I never can see him but I am **heart-burned** an hour after.

HERO: He is of a very melancholy disposition.

BEATRICE: He were an excellent man that were made just in the midway between him and Benedick; the one is too like an image and says nothing, and the other too like my lady's eldest son, evermore tattling.

LEONATO: Then half Signior Benedick's tongue in Count John's mouth, and half Count John's melancholy in Signior Benedick's face –

BEATRICE: With a good leg and a good foot, uncle, and money enough in his purse, such a man would win any woman in the world, if 'a could get her good will.

LEONATO: By my troth, niece, thou wilt never get thee a husband if thou be so shrewd of thy tongue.

ANTONIO: In faith, she's too **curst**.

BEATRICE: Too curst is more than curst. I shall lessen God's sending that way; for it is said, 'God sends a curst cow short horns', but to a cow too curst he sends none.

LEONATO: So, by being too curst, God will send you no horns.

BEATRICE: Just, if he send me no husband; for the which blessing I am at him upon my knees every morning and evening. Lord, I could not endure a husband with a beard on his face! I had rather **lie in the woollen**.

LEONATO: You may light on a husband that hath no beard.

BEATRICE: What should I do with him? Dress him in my apparel and make him my waiting-gentlewoman? He that hath a beard is more than a youth, and he that hath no beard is less than a man; and he that is more than a youth is not for me, and he that is less than a man, I am not for him. Therefore, I will even take sixpence in earnest of the bear-ward, and lead his apes into hell.

LEONATO: Well, then, go you into hell?

BEATRICE: No, but to the gate; and there will the devil meet me, like an old **cuckold**, with horns on his head, and say 'Get you to heaven, Beatrice, get you to heaven; here's no place for you maids.' So deliver I up my apes, and away to Saint Peter for the heavens; he shows me where the bachelors sit, and there live we as merry as the day is long.

ANTONIO: (*to HERO*) Well, niece, I trust you will be ruled by your father.

BEATRICE: Yes, faith; it is my cousin's duty to make curtsy and say, 'Father, as it please you.' But yet for all that,

Leonato urges Hero to accept a marriage proposal from Don Pedro, if she should receive one.

Interestingly, Beatrice's cynical views about marriage are almost exactly the same as Benedick's. Do you think she is protesting too much here, and secretly would love to be married?

Beatrice explains that getting married starts off like an energetic dance, but then becomes slower before speeding up again. Perhaps while making this speech she could demonstrate the dance she is talking about. This will emphasise her own energy and liveliness.

This part of the scene illustrates the theme of disguise literally. All the characters are wearing masks.

Beatrice and Benedick are dancing (with their masks on). They speak as if they do not recognise each other. This would be unlikely, but the pretence is a convenient way for them to find out what each one thinks of the other.

---

cousin, let him be a handsome fellow, or else make another curtsy and say 'Father, as it please me.'

LEONATO: Well, niece, I hope to see you one day fitted with a husband.

BEATRICE: Not till God make men of some other metal than earth. Would it not grieve a woman to be overmastered with a piece of valiant dust? To make an account of her life to a clod of wayward **marl**? No, uncle, I'll none. Adam's sons are my brethren, and, truly, I hold it a sin to match in my kindred.

LEONATO: Daughter, remember what I told you. If the Prince do solicit you in that kind, you know your answer.

BEATRICE: The fault will be in the music, cousin, if you be not wooed in good time. If the Prince be too important, tell him there is measure in every thing and so dance out the answer. For, hear me, Hero: wooing, wedding, and repenting, is as a Scotch jig, a measure, and a cinquepace: the first suit is hot and hasty, like a Scotch jig, and full as fantastical; the wedding, mannerly-modest, as a measure, full of state and ancientry; and then comes repentance and, with his bad legs, falls into the cinquepace faster and faster, till he sink into his grave.

LEONATO: Cousin, you apprehend passing shrewdly.

BEATRICE: I have a good eye, uncle; I can see a church by daylight.

LEONATO: The revellers are entering, brother; make good room.

All put on their masks.

Enter DON PEDRO, CLAUDIO, BENEDICK, DON JOHN, BORACHIO and others, as masquers, with a drummer.

Don Pedro and Hero dance together, with Don Pedro in his 'role' as Claudio. Borachio and Margaret and Antonio and Ursula also dance and joke with one another.

BEATRICE: Will you not tell me who told you so?

BENEDICK: No, you shall pardon me.

BEATRICE: Nor will you not tell me who you are?

BENEDICK: Not now.

BEATRICE: That I was disdainful, and that I had my good wit out of the **'Hundred Merry Tales'** – well this was Signior Benedick that said so.

BENEDICK: What's he?

BEATRICE: I am sure you know him well enough.

BENEDICK: Not I, believe me.

---

marl: topsoil, i.e. earth that is loose and stony

Hundred Merry Tales: a popular book of 16th century humorous tales, each with a moral attached to them

BEATRICE: Did he never make you laugh?

BENEDICK: I pray you, what is he?

BEATRICE: Why, he is the prince's jester: a very dull fool; only his gift is in devising impossible slanders: none but <u>libertines</u> delight in him; and the commendation is not in his wit, but in his villainy; for he both pleases men and angers them, and then they laugh at him and beat him. I am sure he is in the <u>fleet</u>: I would he had <u>boarded me</u>.

BENEDICK: When I know the gentleman, I'll tell him what you say.

BEATRICE: Do, do: <u>he'll but break a comparison or two on me</u>; which, peradventure not marked or not laughed at, strikes him into melancholy; and then there's a partridge wing saved, for the fool will eat no supper that night.

Music.

We must follow the leaders.

BENEDICK: In every good thing.

BEATRICE: Nay, if they lead to any ill, I will leave them at the next turning.

Dance. Then exeunt all except **DON JOHN**, **BORACHIO** *and* **CLAUDIO**.

DON JOHN: Sure my brother is amorous on Hero and hath withdrawn her father to break with him about it. The ladies follow her and but one <u>visor</u> remains.

BORACHIO: And that is Claudio; I know him by his bearing.

DON JOHN: Are not you Signior Benedick?

CLAUDIO: You know me well; I am he.

DON JOHN: Signior, you are very near my brother in his love. He is enamoured on Hero; I pray you, dissuade him from her; she is no equal for his birth. You may do the part of an honest man in it.

CLAUDIO: How know you he loves her?

DON JOHN: I heard him swear his affection.

BORACHIO: So did I too; and he swore he would marry her tonight.

DON JOHN: Come, let us to the banquet.

Exeunt **DON JOHN** *and* **BORACHIO**.

CLAUDIO: Thus answer I in the name of Benedick,
But hear these ill news with the ears of Claudio.
'Tis certain so; the Prince woos for himself.
Friendship is constant in all other things
Save in the office and affairs of love;
Therefore, all hearts in love use their own tongues.
Let every eye negotiate for itself,
And trust no agent; for beauty is a witch
Against whose charms faith melteth into blood.
This is an accident of hourly proof,
Which I mistrusted not. Farewell, therefore, Hero!

Exit.

Beatrice calls Benedick 'the prince's jester'. This suggests that his favourite role is to be the centre of attention, making people laugh. It also hints that he acts like a fool just to stay in favour with the Prince (Don Pedro).

Beatrice has the upper hand in this conversation. She is able to be very critical of Benedick, in a joking way, and can get away with it. Benedick cannot answer her back, since he is pretending to be someone else!

Don John is spreading malicious gossip here. Not only does he say that Don Pedro is in love with Hero, he also claims that she is not good enough for such a match. He knows he is actually talking to Claudio, but behaves as though he is having a conversation with Benedick.

This SOLILOQUY relays Claudio's thoughts to the audience. Shakespeare shows how important this speech is by presenting it in BLANK VERSE. The rest of the scene is in prose.

The speech is full of words connected to gossip: 'ill news', 'tongues' 'negotiate'. Claudio decides to change his mind about Hero following Don John's comments. This does not show him in a very good light – if he can fall out of love so quickly, it suggests that he does not really love her.

<u>libertines:</u> rogues with no morals
<u>fleet:</u> she means the company of guests (she is using a sailing metaphor)
<u>boarded me:</u> talked to me/danced with me
<u>he'll but break a comparison or two on me:</u> he'll just call me a few rude names
<u>visor:</u> a person who is wearing a mask

Benedick, having seen Don Pedro dance with Hero, gets the wrong idea and thinks that he is wooing Hero for himself. Benedick sees that Claudio is miserable and thinks this is why. He does not know about the sly things Don John has just said. Benedick also takes the opportunity to speak to Don Pedro about Beatrice's horrible words. He says that he will have his revenge, but he seems upset that she does not really know him very well. He obviously worries about her and what she thinks of him.

This is a mysterious line from Beatrice. It suggests that she and Benedick have been a couple before and that, for some reason, Benedick called it off. There is nothing else in the play to suggest this, however.

Beatrice is perceptive here. She thinks that Claudio's misery is due to jealousy.

Don Pedro resolves the first set of confusions and conflict in the play by confirming that he has been proposing to Hero in Claudio's name. He tells Claudio that Hero is happy to marry him and he wishes his friend much joy in his forthcoming marriage.

Claudio and Hero need to kiss here to signify to the audience that the tension has been sorted out and that things are happy between these two characters.

wherefore: why

blazon: interpretation, words (usually found on a shield)

dote: love dearly

DON PEDRO: Come, lady, come; you have lost the heart of Signior Benedick.

BEATRICE: Indeed, my lord, he lent it me awhile, and I gave him use for it, a double heart for his single one. Marry, once before he won it of me with false dice, therefore your grace may well say I have lost it.

DON PEDRO: You have put him down, lady, you have put him down.

BEATRICE: So I would not he should do me, my lord, lest I should prove the mother of fools. I have brought Count Claudio, whom you sent me to seek.

DON PEDRO: Why, how now, Count! <u>Wherefore</u> are you sad?

CLAUDIO: Not sad, my lord.

DON PEDRO: How then? Sick?

CLAUDIO: Neither, my lord.

BEATRICE: The Count is neither sad, nor sick, nor merry, nor well; but civil count, civil as an orange, and something of that jealous complexion.

DON PEDRO: I' faith, lady, I think your <u>blazon</u> to be true, though, I'll be sworn, if he be so, his conceit is false. Here, Claudio, I have wooed in thy name, and fair Hero is won. I have broke with her father, and his good will obtained; name the day of marriage, and God give thee joy!

LEONATO: Count, take of me my daughter, and with her my fortunes. His grace hath made the match, and all Grace say Amen to it!

BEATRICE: Speak, Count, 'tis your cue.

CLAUDIO: Silence is the perfectest herald of joy; I were but little happy, if I could say how much. Lady, as you are mine, I am yours; I give away myself for you and <u>dote</u> upon the exchange.

BEATRICE: Speak, cousin; or, if you cannot, stop his mouth with a kiss, and let not him speak neither.

DON PEDRO: In faith, lady, you have a merry heart.

BEATRICE: Yea, my lord; I thank it, poor fool, it keeps on the windy side of care. My cousin tells him in his ear that he is in her heart.

CLAUDIO: And so she doth, cousin.

BEATRICE: Good Lord, for alliance! Thus goes every one to the world but I, and I am sunburnt; I may sit in a corner and cry '<u>Heigh-ho</u> for a husband!'

DON PEDRO: Lady Beatrice, I will get you one.

BEATRICE: I would rather have one of your father's getting. Hath your grace ne'er a brother like you? Your father got excellent husbands, if a maid could come by them.

DON PEDRO: Will you have me, lady?

BEATRICE: No, my lord, unless I might have another for working-days: your grace is too costly to wear every day. But, I beseech your grace, pardon me: I was born to speak all mirth and no matter.

DON PEDRO: Your silence most offends me, and to be merry best becomes you; for, out of question, you were born in a merry hour.

BEATRICE: No, sure, my lord, my mother cried; but then there was a star danced, and under that was I born. Cousins, God give you joy!

LEONATO: Niece, will you look to those things I told you of?

BEATRICE: I cry you mercy, uncle. By your grace's pardon.

Exit.

DON PEDRO: By my troth, a pleasant-spirited lady.

LEONATO: There's little of the melancholy element in her, my lord; she is never sad but when she sleeps, and not ever sad then; for I have heard my daughter say, she hath often dreamed of unhappiness and waked herself with laughing.

DON PEDRO: She cannot endure to hear tell of a husband.

LEONATO: O, by no means; she mocks all her wooers out of suit.

DON PEDRO: She were an excellent wife for Benedick.

LEONATO: O Lord, my lord, if they were but a week married, they would talk themselves mad.

DON PEDRO: County Claudio, when mean you to go to church?

CLAUDIO: To-morrow, my lord. Time goes on crutches till love have all his rites.

LEONATO: Not till Monday, my dear son, which is hence a just seven-night; and a time too brief, too, to have all things answer my mind.

DON PEDRO: Come, you shake the head at so long a breathing; but, I warrant thee, Claudio, the time shall not go dully by us. I will in the interim undertake one of <u>Hercules' labours</u>; which is, to bring Signior Benedick and the Lady Beatrice into a mountain of affection the one with the other. I would fain have it a match, and I doubt not but to fashion it, if you three will but minister such assistance as I shall give you direction.

After Beatrice moans that everyone is getting married but her, the Prince asks her to marry him. She refuses, saying she would also need a husband for 'every day' because Don Pedro is too grand for her. She uses a metaphor of clothing, comparing Don Pedro to fine smart clothes, while for a husband she would need something more practical and casual. This is one of several clothing images in the play.

Beatrice leaves the stage and the Prince comments that she is a happy, cheerful character. Leonato agrees, saying that she never seems to be sad, and even if she has a bad dream she wakes up feeling happy.

Don Pedro comments that Beatrice would be a perfect partner for Benedick. Leonato is less convinced, saying they would drive each other mad within a week of being married.

Not wishing to delay, Claudio says that he wants the marriage to take place the very next day. Leonato says it will be in seven days' time.

Don Pedro introduces the next storyline – he intends to find a way to get Beatrice and Benedick to fall in love with each other. He asks Claudio, Hero and Leonato for help.

heigh-ho: oh well

Hercules' labours: the Greek hero Hercules had to undertake a series of difficult challenges

LEONATO: My lord, I am for you, though it cost me ten nights' watchings.

CLAUDIO: And I, my lord.

DON PEDRO: And you too, gentle Hero?

HERO: I will do any modest **office**, my lord, to help my cousin to a good husband.

DON PEDRO: And Benedick is not the unhopefullest husband that I know. Thus far can I praise him: he is of a noble strain, of approved valour and confirmed honesty. I will teach you how to humour your cousin, that she shall fall in love with Benedick; and I, with your two helps, will so practise on Benedick that, in despite of his quick wit and his queasy stomach, he shall fall in love with Beatrice. If we can do this, Cupid is no longer an archer; his glory shall be ours, for we are the only love-gods. Go in with me, and I will tell you my drift.

Exeunt.

The scene ends in a happy, romantic mood. Two of the main characters are engaged to be married and there are plans for two others to find love. Don Pedro's final speech is full of references to romance: 'Cupid', 'Love-gods', 'fall in love', etc.

Scene 2 is in direct contrast to the previous scene. The talk is still of marriage, but the tone is darker as Don John reveals his plans.

SCENE 2. *LEONATO's house.*

Enter DON JOHN and BORACHIO.

DON JOHN: It is so; the Count Claudio shall marry the daughter of Leonato.

BORACHIO: Yea, my lord, but I can **cross** it.

DON JOHN: Any **bar**, any cross, any impediment will be medicinable to me: I am sick in displeasure to him, and whatsoever comes athwart his affection ranges evenly with mine. How canst thou cross this marriage?

BORACHIO: Not honestly, my lord; but so covertly that no dishonesty shall appear in me.

DON JOHN: Show me briefly how.

Borachio reminds Don John that he has been very close to Hero's maid, Margaret, for the past year. He tells Don John that he can arrange for a secret lover's meeting with her in front of Hero's bedroom window. When Margaret and Borachio are embracing, he will use Hero's name, so people will think that Hero is being unfaithful.

BORACHIO: I think I told your lordship a year since, how much I am in the favour of Margaret, the waiting gentlewoman to Hero.

DON JOHN: I remember.

BORACHIO: I can, at any unseasonable instant of the night, appoint her to look out at her lady's chamber window.

DON JOHN: What life is in that, to be the death of this marriage?

BORACHIO: The poison of that lies in you to temper. Go you to the Prince your brother; spare not to tell him that he hath wronged his honour in marrying the renowned Claudio – whose estimation do you mightily hold up – to a contaminated stale, such a one as Hero.

DON JOHN: What proof shall I make of that?

BORACHIO: Proof enough to misuse the Prince, to vex Claudio, to undo Hero and kill Leonato. Look you for any other issue?

DON JOHN: Only to despite them I will endeavour any thing.

office: duty, task

cross: prevent

bar: obstacle

BORACHIO: Go, then; find me a meet hour to draw Don Pedro and the Count Claudio alone. Tell them that you know that Hero loves me; intend a kind of zeal both to the Prince and Claudio – as in love of your brother's honour, who hath made this match, and his friend's reputation, who is thus like to be <u>cozened</u> with the semblance of a maid – that you have discovered thus. They will scarcely believe this without <u>trial</u>; offer them instances, which shall bear no less likelihood than to see me at her chamber window, hear me call Margaret Hero, hear Margaret term me Claudio; and bring them to see this the very night before the intended wedding – for in the meantime I will so fashion the matter that Hero shall be absent – and there shall appear such seeming truth of Hero's disloyalty that jealousy shall be called assurance, and all the preparation overthrown.

DON JOHN: Grow this to what adverse issue it can, I will put it in practise. Be cunning in the working this, and thy fee is a thousand ducats.

BORACHIO: Be you constant in the accusation, and my cunning shall not shame me.

DON JOHN: I will presently go learn their day of marriage.

Exeunt.

The theme of confusion runs through the play. People frequently overhear information and get the wrong idea. There are also many cases of mistaken identity caused by people hiding, wearing masks and disguises, or – as in this case – deliberately playing a role.

Borachio has planned for the deception to take place the night before the wedding. This will give their scheme the maximum shock value, but it will also mean that there is very little time for the confusion to be sorted out. As a result, the wedding will almost certainly not take place.

Don John is so delighted with Borachio's plan that he agrees to pay him a huge fee if everything works out.

Scene 3. **LEONATO'S** *orchard.*

Enter **BENEDICK**.

BENEDICK: Boy!

Enter **BOY**.

BOY: Signior?

BENEDICK: In my chamber window lies a book; bring it hither to me in the orchard.

BOY: I am here already, sir.

BENEDICK: I know that; but I would have thee hence, and here again.

Exit **BOY**.

I do much wonder that one man, seeing how much another man is a fool when he dedicates his <u>behaviours</u> to love, will, after he hath laughed at such shallow follies in others, become the argument of his own scorn by falling in love; and such a man is Claudio. I have known when there was no music with him but the drum and the <u>fife</u>, and now had he rather hear the <u>tabour</u> and the pipe. I have known when he would have walked ten mile afoot to see a good armour, and now will he lie ten nights awake, carving the fashion of a new <u>doublet</u>. He was wont to speak plain and to the purpose, like an honest man and a soldier, and now is he turned <u>orthography</u>; his words are a very fantastical banquet, just so many strange dishes. May I be so

This scene takes place in the sunshine and pleasant atmosphere of an Italian orchard. The setting would immediately lift the atmosphere, visually, compared to the secluded, dark plotting of the previous scene.

This speech is a SOLILOQUY, a dramatic device where a character talks out loud while they are alone. Soliloquies often allow an audience to find out what a character is thinking. In this case, Benedick wonders how a man could possibly fall in love after seeing what fools love makes of people. He remarks that Claudio seems obsessed, lying awake, wearing new clothes and talking in a romantic fashion, instead of acting like a proper soldier.

<u>cozened</u>: cheated, deceived
<u>trial</u>: proof
<u>behaviours</u>: actions
<u>fife</u>: a small flute-like instrument
<u>tabour</u>: small drum used for dancing
<u>doublet</u>: waistcoat
<u>orthography</u>: speaking in a very stylish, polished way

Ironically, Benedick fails to realise that he could be talking about himself. Instead of being engaged in soldier's duties, he is pacing up and down the garden thinking about falling in love!

Here Benedick tempts fate again by declaring that he will never be made a fool by falling love. He believes he will never find a woman who has all the qualities he is looking for in a partner.

When he sees Don Pedro and Claudio, Benedick hides behind one of the trees. The audience should still be able to see him listening to the other characters, but Benedick believes he is hidden from view. Of course, the others know he is there and they intend him to overhear everything they say.

Music is always very important in Shakespearean comedies. In this case it would be used as a backdrop to the romantic 'trick', keeping the mood light. It is important that you appreciate the difference between this trick and the one being planned by Don John. This deception is designed to have a happy ending, while Don John's plan is used only for destruction and harm. The music helps to make this distinction more obvious.

Ironically, Balthasar's song begins with lyrics about men who deceive and who commit fraud. This is one of the strongest themes running throughout the play.

Monsieur Love: Claudio
crotchets: strange ideas
sheeps' guts: violin strings
bonny: beautiful

converted and see with these eyes? I cannot tell; I think not. I will not be sworn but love may transform me to an oyster; but I'll take my oath on it, till he have made an oyster of me, he shall never make me such a fool. One woman is fair, yet I am well; another is wise, yet I am well; another virtuous, yet I am well; but till all graces be in one woman, one woman shall not come in my grace. Rich she shall be, that's certain; wise, or I'll none; virtuous, or I'll never cheapen her; fair, or I'll never look on her; mild, or come not near me; noble, or not I for an angel; of good discourse, an excellent musician, and her hair shall be of what colour it please God. Ha! The Prince and **Monsieur Love**! I will hide me in the arbour.

Withdraws.

Enter DON PEDRO, CLAUDIO *and* LEONATO.
DON PEDRO: Come, shall we hear this music?
CLAUDIO: Yea, my good lord. How still the evening is,
As hush'd on purpose to grace harmony!
DON PEDRO: See you where Benedick hath hid himself?
CLAUDIO: O, very well, my lord; the music ended,
We'll fit the kid-fox with a pennyworth.

Enter BALTHASAR *with music.*
DON PEDRO: Come, Balthasar, we'll hear that song again.
BALTHASAR: O, good my lord, tax not so bad a voice
To slander music any more than once.
DON PEDRO: It is the witness still of excellency
To put a strange face on his own perfection.
I pray thee, sing, and let me woo no more.
BALTHASAR: Because you talk of wooing, I will sing;
Since many a wooer doth commence his suit
To her he thinks not worthy; yet he woos,
Yet will he swear he loves.
DON PEDRO: Now, pray thee, come;
Or, if thou wilt hold longer argument,
Do it in notes.
BALTHASAR: Note this before my notes;
There's not a note of mine that's worth the noting.
DON PEDRO: Why, these are very **crotchets** that he speaks;
Note, notes, forsooth, and nothing.
Music.
BENEDICK: Now, divine air! Now is his soul ravished! Is it not strange that **sheep's guts** should hale souls out of men's bodies? Well, a horn for my money, when all's done.
BALTHASAR *sings.*
　　　Sigh no more, ladies, sigh no more,
　　　　Men were deceivers ever,
　　　One foot in sea and one on shore,
　　　　To one thing constant never:
　　　Then sigh not so, but let them go,
　　　　And be you blithe and **bonny**,
　　　Converting all your sounds of woe
　　　　Into Hey nonny, nonny.

Sing no more ditties, sing no moe,
Of dumps so dull and heavy;
The fraud of men was ever so,
Since summer first was leafy:
Then sigh not so, &c.

DON PEDRO: By my troth, a good song.

BALTHASAR: And an ill singer, my lord.

DON PEDRO: Ha, no, no, faith; thou singest well enough for a shift.

BENEDICK: An he had been a dog that should have howled thus, they would have hanged him; and I pray God his bad voice bode no mischief. I had as lief have heard the night-raven, come what plague could have come after it.

DON PEDRO: Yea, marry, dost thou hear, Balthasar? I pray thee, get us some excellent music; for tomorrow night we would have it at the Lady Hero's chamber window.

BALTHASAR: The best I can, my lord.

DON PEDRO: Do so; farewell.

Exit BALTHASAR.

Come hither, Leonato. What was it you told me of today, that your niece Beatrice was in love with Signior Benedick?

CLAUDIO: O, ay: stalk on, stalk on; the fowl sits. I did never think that lady would have loved any man.

LEONATO: No, nor I neither; but most wonderful that she should so dote on Signior Benedick, whom she hath in all outward behaviors seemed ever to abhor.

BENEDICK: Is't possible? Sits the wind in that corner?

LEONATO: By my troth, my lord, I cannot tell what to think of it; but that she loves him with an enraged affection, it is past the infinite of thought.

DON PEDRO: May be she doth but **counterfeit**.

CLAUDIO: Faith, like enough.

LEONATO: O God, counterfeit! There was never counterfeit of passion came so near the life of passion as she discovers it.

DON PEDRO: Why, what effects of passion shows she?

CLAUDIO: Bait the hook well; this fish will bite.

LEONATO: What effects, my lord? She will sit you – you heard my daughter tell you how.

CLAUDIO: She did, indeed.

DON PEDRO: How, how, I pray you? You amaze me; I would have thought her spirit had been invincible against all assaults of affection.

LEONATO: I would have sworn it had, my lord; especially against Benedick.

BENEDICK: I should think this a **gull**, but that the white-bearded fellow speaks it; **knavery** cannot, sure, hide himself in such reverence.

CLAUDIO: He hath ta'en the infection: hold it up.

DON PEDRO: Hath she made her affection known to Benedick?

Benedick is talking to himself here, as he is hidden within the orchard. Even though the song was good, he is determined to remain grumpy and says that Balthasar sings worse than a howling dog.

Don Pedro begins his plan by asking Leonato if he has heard the latest gossip: Beatrice is in love with Benedick. Claudio plays along, saying that he did not think it possible that Beatrice could love any man.

While the others are discussing Beatrice and Benedick, Benedick is chipping in with his own thoughts. Remember that these are for the benefit of the audience because the others are not supposed to be able to hear him.

Benedick says that he would think this news was a trick, if it were not for the fact that Leonato is involved. Benedick trusts Leonato's age, honour and wisdom, and so believes the information utterly.

counterfeit: pretend
gull: hoax
knavery: trickery

According to Claudio, Beatrice has confided in Hero and has said that she could never write and tell Benedick that she loves him after spending so much time being nasty to him. Apparently, Beatrice spends half the night lying awake and wondering what to do about this situation.

Notice the verbs that Claudio uses to describe Beatrice's actions: 'weeps', 'sobs', 'prays'. This is exactly the type of foolish behaviour that Benedick says he despises in people such as Claudio, who suddenly act in a strange way because they are in love.

In order to ensure that their plan works, Claudio points out that Benedick would be bound to make fun of Beatrice if he were to find out. (Overhearing this, Benedick would naturally start to wonder about how he really would behave.)

Don Pedro also points out Beatrice's virtues, detailing all her positive qualities. Claudio agrees that the only thing she is not sensible about is the way she feels about Benedick.

The idea that a person could die from unrequited love was a popular one during Tudor times and in earlier romances. It was generally believed that true love was so powerful that it could affect a person like a kind of sickness or fever. The audience at this time, as well as the characters in the play, would have quite happily believed that a person really could die from a broken heart.

halfpence: tiny pieces
railed: ranted
flout: insult
ecstasy: madness
afeared: frightened
daffed: put aside

LEONATO: No, and swears she never will; that's her torment.

CLAUDIO: 'Tis true, indeed, so your daughter says, 'Shall I,' says she, 'that have so oft encountered him with scorn, write to him that I love him?'

LEONATO: This says she now when she is beginning to write to him; for she'll be up twenty times a night, and there will she sit in her smock till she have writ a sheet of paper. My daughter tells us all.

CLAUDIO: Now you talk of a sheet of paper, I remember a pretty jest your daughter told us of.

LEONATO: O, when she had writ it and was reading it over, she found Benedick and Beatrice between the sheet?

CLAUDIO: That.

LEONATO: O, she tore the letter into a thousand **halfpence**; **railed** at herself, that she should be so immodest to write to one that she knew would **flout** her. 'I measure him,' says she, 'by my own spirit; for I should flout him, if he writ to me; yea, though I love him, I should.'

CLAUDIO: Then down upon her knees she falls, weeps, sobs, beats her heart, tears her hair, prays, curses – 'O sweet Benedick! God give me patience!'

LEONATO: She doth indeed, my daughter says so; and the **ecstasy** hath so much overborne her that my daughter is sometime **afeared** she will do a desperate outrage to herself. It is very true.

DON PEDRO: It were good that Benedick knew of it by some other, if she will not discover it.

CLAUDIO: To what end? He would make but a sport of it and torment the poor lady worse.

DON PEDRO: An he should, it were an alms to hang him. She's an excellent sweet lady; and, out of all suspicion, she is virtuous.

CLAUDIO: And she is exceeding wise.

DON PEDRO: In every thing but in loving Benedick.

LEONATO: O, my lord, wisdom and blood combating in so tender a body, we have ten proofs to one that blood hath the victory. I am sorry for her, as I have just cause, being her uncle and her guardian.

DON PEDRO: I would she had bestowed this dotage on me; I would have **daffed** all other respects and made her half myself. I pray you, tell Benedick of it, and hear what 'a will say.

LEONATO: Were it good, think you?

CLAUDIO: Hero thinks surely she will die; for she says she will die, if he love her not; and she will die, ere she make her love known; and she will die, if he woo her, rather than she will bate one breath of her accustomed crossness.

DON PEDRO: She doth well. If she should make tender of her love, 'tis very possible he'll scorn it; for the man, as you know all, hath a contemptible spirit.

CLAUDIO: He is a very proper man.

DON PEDRO: He hath, indeed, a good outward happiness.

CLAUDIO: Before God, and in my mind, very wise.

DON PEDRO: He doth, indeed, show some sparks that are like wit.

CLAUDIO: And I take him to be valiant.

DON PEDRO: As <u>Hector</u>, I assure you; and in the managing of quarrels you may say he is wise, for either he avoids them with great discretion, or undertakes them with a most Christian-like fear.

LEONATO: If he do fear God, 'a must necessarily keep peace; if he break the peace, he ought to enter into a quarrel with fear and trembling.

DON PEDRO: And so will he do; for the man doth fear God, howsoever it seems not in him by some large jests he will make. Well, I am sorry for your niece. Shall we go seek Benedick, and tell him of her love?

CLAUDIO: Never tell him, my lord; let her wear it out with good <u>counsel</u>.

LEONATO: Nay, that's impossible; she may wear her heart out first.

DON PEDRO: Well, we will hear further of it by your daughter; let it cool the while. I love Benedick well; and I could wish he would modestly examine himself, to see how much he is unworthy so good a lady.

LEONATO: My lord, will you walk? Dinner is ready.

CLAUDIO: If he do not dote on her upon this, I will never trust my expectation.

DON PEDRO: Let there be the same net spread for her; and that must your daughter and her gentlewomen carry. The sport will be, when they hold one an opinion of another's <u>dotage</u>, and no such matter; that's the scene that I would see, which will be merely a dumb-show. Let us send her to call him in to dinner.

Exeunt DON PEDRO, CLAUDIO and LEONATO.

BENEDICK: (*coming forward*) This can be no trick. The conference was sadly borne. They have the truth of this from Hero. They seem to pity the lady; it seems her affections have their <u>full bent</u>. Love me? Why, it must be requited. I hear how I am <u>censured</u>: they say I will bear myself proudly, if I perceive the love come from her; they say too that she will rather die than give any sign of affection. I did never think to marry. I must not seem proud; happy are they that hear their detractions and can put them to mending. They say the lady is fair; 'tis a truth, I can bear them witness; and virtuous; 'tis so, I cannot reprove it; and wise, but for loving me; by my troth, it is no addition to her wit, nor no great argument of her folly, for I will be <u>horribly</u> in love with her. I may chance have some odd quirks and remnants of wit broken on me, because I have railed so long against marriage; but doth not the appetite alter? A man loves the meat in his youth that he cannot endure in his age.

Cleverly, Don Pedro and Claudio now start talking about Benedick's good points. Remember that Benedick is still listening in on their conversation, so he would feel flattered and even more inclined to believe what they are saying.

The imagery here is important, with words connected to love being used alongside words connected to fighting. These are two strong ideas running through the play.

This part of the plan is very devious. Even though the men know that Benedick is listening to every word, they consider whether they should tell him about this news. Claudio pretends to be shocked and Don Pedro agrees that they should wait for a while before taking the matter further.

All the other characters now exit the stage, leaving Benedick to think aloud about what he has just heard.

After hearing Don Pedro's and Claudio's words, Benedick now realises that Beatrice has all the qualities that he could possibly want in a partner. She is beautiful, virtuous and intelligent.

The phrase 'horribly in love' is interesting to a modern audience because it suggests that sometimes being in love with a person can be an unpleasant experience, particularly if the love is not returned. For a confirmed bachelor, the whole idea might indeed be quite frightening. However, Benedick is falling in love with no holds barred, which is what the phrase implied at that time.

<u>Hector:</u> a Trojan soldier, famed for his bravery and skill in battle

<u>counsel:</u> decision

<u>dotage:</u> love

<u>full bent:</u> as far as they can go

<u>censured:</u> to give an opinion about

<u>horribly:</u> exceedingly

Benedick reflects on his earlier words (when he said that he would die a bachelor). He now claims that he didn't mean he would never WANT to get married, but that he simply thought he would get so old he would die first. It sounds like he is trying to convince himself.

Beatrice's entrance is very important because the audience will be looking to see how Benedick treats her. After all, he now believes that she is desperately, but secretly, in love with him.

Even though Beatrice only invites him in for dinner and does not treat him any differently from before, Benedick analyses every word she says to him, searching for signs of her affection. He calls her 'fair Beatrice' and thanks her profusely for the trouble she has gone to. Beatrice seems a bit confused by this change in him and explains that it was no trouble.

After Beatrice leaves, Benedick finds subtle meaning in all her words to back up his view that she is in love with him. He really manages to convince himself, which shows that any words can easily be confused. People who want to believe something will find evidence in the simplest sentence. The play is full of such examples of confusion.

Shall quips and sentences and these paper bullets of the brain awe a man from the career of his humour? No, the world must be peopled. When I said I would die a bachelor, I did not think I should live till I were married. Here comes Beatrice. By this day! she's a fair lady: I do spy some marks of love in her.

Enter BEATRICE.

BEATRICE: Against my will I am sent to bid you come in to dinner.

BENEDICK: Fair Beatrice, I thank you for your pains.

BEATRICE: I took no more pains for those thanks than you take pains to thank me; if it had been painful, I would not have come.

BENEDICK: You take pleasure then in the message?

BEATRICE: Yea, just so much as you may take upon a knife's point and choke a <u>daw</u> withal. You have no stomach, signior; fare you well.

Exit.

BENEDICK: Ha! 'Against my will I am sent to bid you come in to dinner;' – there's a double meaning in that. 'I took no more pains for those thanks than you took pains to thank me' – that's as much as to say, 'Any pains that I take for you is as easy as thanks.' If I do not take pity of her, I am a villain; if I do not love her, I am a Jew. I will go get her picture.

Exit.

<u>daw:</u> a fool

40

ACT 2 QUESTIONS

Understanding the plot

1. What does Beatrice say would make a perfect man?
2. Why does Leonato believe Beatrice will never get married?
3. How does Beatrice insult Benedick at the party?
4. Where does Benedick overhear a conversation about Beatrice being in love with him?
5. What makes Benedick believe what he is hearing?

Who says this?

1. 'I can never see him but I am heart-burned an hour after?'
2. 'I could not endure a husband with a beard.'
3. 'I heard him swear his affection.'
4. 'She speaks poniards and every word stabs.'
5. 'Bait the hook well, this fish will bite.'

Name the character

1. Who agrees to woo Hero on Claudio's behalf?
2. Who does Claudio pretend to be at the party?
3. Who is enraged at Claudio's wedding plans?
4. Who has been in a relationship with Borachio for over a year?
5. Who has apparently been tearing letters into shreds and pacing about all night?

Understanding character

1. Why does Don John make Beatrice feel uneasy?
2. Who becomes jealous of Don Pedro?
3. Who helps to clear up the wooing misunderstanding?
4. Why does Beatrice refuse Don Pedro's marriage proposal?
5. Who thinks up the nasty plan involving Hero's 'adultery'?

Themes and imagery

1. Appearance/reality: Why is the masked ball an effective dramatic device?
2. Love: According to Benedick, what are lovers obsessed by?
3. Fighting: Who feels as though he has been stabbed and had an army firing at him?
4. What does the phrase 'court Jester' suggest about Benedick's character?
5. What is the significance of the 'willow-tree' imagery?

ACT 3 SUMMARY

ACT 3

Hero, *URSULA* and Margaret are planning together in the orchard. Margaret is sent to tell Beatrice that her friends are talking about her. When Beatrice arrives she falls into the trap and hides nearby, as intended. She overhears Hero and Ursula talking about Benedick's excellent qualities and reputation. By contrast, she hears herself described as proud and stubborn. Hero even says that she will try to talk Benedick out of his love for Beatrice, as she knows Beatrice would never return it. Beatrice is taken in by Hero's clever reverse-psychology and starts to think that she will return Benedick's love.

While chatting to Claudio, Benedick and Leonato, Don Pedro reveals that he intends to return to Arragon after Claudio's marriage. Benedick announces that he is a changed man. Don Pedro and Claudio mock him, realising that he is desperately in love and acting just like the young men he moaned about in the previous Act. Benedick leaves with Leonato, probably to discuss marrying Beatrice. Don John interrupts to tell Claudio and Don Pedro about Hero's 'affair' with Borachio. If they get proof, Claudio and Don Pedro plan to disgrace Hero in public at the wedding the next morning.

Out on the streets of Messina, *DOGBERRY*, *VERGES* and the rest of the nightwatchmen patrol the area. Dogberry is unintentionally funny as he tells

the nightwatchmen about their duties. However, he is also unintentionally smart. Realising that Leonato's house is busy due to the wedding there the next say, Dogberry puts the Watch on their guard. As they are talking, Borachio appears looking for Conrade. In ear-shot of the nightwatchmen, Borachio boasts about what a villain he is. He explains that he has just earned lots of money from Don John for embracing Margaret and pretending she was Hero while Claudio and Don Pedro watched. The nightwatchmen arrest Borachio and Conrade for their deeds.

Hero, Margaret and Ursula gossip about Hero's wedding dress. Beatrice comes on stage and the women realise she is madly in love with Benedick but not sure what to do about her feelings.

Dogberry and Verges visit Leonato to tell him about the arrest they have made. They frustrate Leonato, however, by not coming to the point, so he tells them to question the captives themselves and give him some peace before his daughter's wedding.

KEY TO THEMES

 love

 disguise/appearance versus reality

 nature

 gossip/overhearing

 food

 director's notes

 fighting

 marriage

 clothing

 honour

This is a parallel scene to the one which has just taken place with Benedick. Hero, Margaret and Ursula are plotting how they can lure Beatrice into the garden so she can 'overhear' them talking about Benedick's love for her.

Note that the light tone is again symbolised by the action being outside in the sunshine.

The romantic subject of this scene is emphasised by the vocabulary. Hero talks of sweet-smelling flowers and the sun.

Hero takes the lead in this scene, explaining to the other ladies that they must be overheard gossiping entirely about Benedick and his love for Beatrice. They plan for Beatrice to overhear everything.

Ursula uses a fishing metaphor. She refers to Beatrice as the fish, implying that they intend to catch her with their bait – in other words, she will fall for their trap. Note that Claudio used the same metaphor in the parallel scene involving Benedick ('Bait the hook well; this fish will bite', Act 2 Scene 3).

pleached: hedges which interlock at the top

bower: a shady, leafy shelter

coverture: a sheltered place

haggards: a peregrine falcon

ACT 3

SCENE 1. LEONATO's garden.

Enter HERO, MARGARET and URSULA.

HERO: Good Margaret, run thee to the parlour;
  There shalt thou find my cousin Beatrice
  Proposing with the Prince and Claudio.
  Whisper her ear, and tell her I and Ursula
  Walk in the orchard, and our whole discourse
  Is all of her; say that thou overheard'st us,
  And bid her steal into the **pleached** bower,
  Where honeysuckles, ripen'd by the sun,
  Forbid the sun to enter – like favourites,
  Made proud by princes, that advance their pride
  Against that power that bred it. There will she hide her,
  To listen our purpose. This is thy office;
  Bear thee well in it and leave us alone.

MARGARET: I'll make her come, I warrant you,
  presently.

Exit.

HERO: Now, Ursula, when Beatrice doth come,
  As we do trace this alley up and down,
  Our talk must only be of Benedick.
  When I do name him, let it be thy part
  To praise him more than ever man did merit.
  My talk to thee must be how Benedick
  Is sick in love with Beatrice. Of this matter
  Is little Cupid's crafty arrow made,
  That only wounds by hearsay. Now begin;

Enter BEATRICE, behind.

  For look where Beatrice, like a lapwing, runs
  Close by the ground, to hear our conference.

URSULA: The pleasant'st angling is to see the fish
  Cut with her golden oars the silver stream,
  And greedily devour the treacherous bait;
  So angle we for Beatrice, who even now
  Is couched in the woodbine **coverture**.
  Fear you not my part of the dialogue.

HERO: Then go we near her, that her ear lose nothing
  Of the false sweet bait that we lay for it.

They approach the bower.

  No, truly, Ursula, she is too disdainful;
  I know her spirits are as coy and wild
  As **haggards** of the rock.

URSULA: But are you sure
  That Benedick loves Beatrice so entirely?

HERO: So says the Prince and my new-trothed lord.

URSULA: And did they bid you tell her of it, madam?

HERO: They did entreat me to acquaint her of it;
  But I persuaded them, if they loved Benedick,

Ursula claims to think that Beatrice isn't good enough for Benedick. Hero agrees that Beatrice is too proud and thinks too much of herself to ever fall in love.

Remember that Beatrice is listening to this conversation. Everything that Hero and Ursula say is designed to make her think about falling in love with Benedick. This is exactly the same trick that Claudio and Don Pedro played so successfully.

Hero takes great care to point out all Benedick's good points. She then spends far longer talking about Beatrice's bad points. She is making Beatrice sound very unreasonable – and the only way for Beatrice to prove her wrong is by loving Benedick!

Notice how often the theme of love and the theme of fighting appear together. In this speech, Hero says that she plans to tell Benedick to fight against his love.

agate … vilely cut: an agate is a carved stone, in this case it has a man carved on it; a 'vilely cut' agate is not well carved

slanders: lies

44

To wish him wrestle with affection,
And never to let Beatrice know of it.
URSULA: Why did you so? Doth not the gentleman
Deserve as full as fortunate a bed
As ever Beatrice shall couch upon?
HERO: O god of love! I know he doth deserve
As much as may be yielded to a man;
But Nature never framed a woman's heart
Of prouder stuff than that of Beatrice.
Disdain and scorn ride sparkling in her eyes,
Misprising what they look on, and her wit
Values itself so highly that to her
All matter else seems weak. She cannot love,
Nor take no shape nor project of affection,
She is so self-endeared.
URSULA: Sure, I think so;
And therefore, certainly, it were not good
She knew his love, lest she make sport at it.
HERO: Why, you speak truth. I never yet saw man,
How wise, how noble, young, how rarely featured,
But she would spell him backward. If fair-faced,
She would swear the gentleman should be her sister;
If black, why, Nature, drawing of an antique,
Made a foul blot; if tall, a lance ill-headed;
If low, an **agate** very **vilely cut**;
If speaking, why, a vane blown with all winds;
If silent, why, a block moved with none.
So turns she every man the wrong side out,
And never gives to truth and virtue that
Which simpleness and merit purchaseth.
URSULA: Sure, sure, such carping is not commendable.
HERO: No, not to be so odd and from all fashions
As Beatrice is, cannot be commendable;
But who dare tell her so? If I should speak,
She would mock me into air; O, she would laugh me
Out of myself, press me to death with wit!
Therefore let Benedick, like cover'd fire,
Consume away in sighs, waste inwardly.
It were a better death than die with mocks,
Which is as bad as die with tickling.
URSULA: Yet tell her of it; hear what she will say.
HERO: No; rather I will go to Benedick
And counsel him to fight against his passion.
And, truly, I'll devise some honest **slanders**
To stain my cousin with. One doth not know
How much an ill word may empoison liking.
URSULA: O, do not do your cousin such a wrong.
She cannot be so much without true judgment –
Having so swift and excellent a wit
As she is prized to have – as to refuse
So rare a gentleman as Signior Benedick.
HERO: He is the only man of Italy.
Always excepted my dear Claudio.

URSULA: I pray you, be not angry with me, madam,
Speaking my fancy: Signior Benedick,
For shape, for bearing, argument and valour,
Goes foremost in report through Italy.
HERO: Indeed, he hath an excellent good name.
URSULA: His excellence did earn it, ere he had it.
When are you married, madam?
HERO: Why, every day, tomorrow. Come, go in;
I'll show thee some attires, and have thy counsel
Which is the best to furnish me tomorrow.
URSULA: She's <u>limed</u>, I warrant you; we have caught her,
madam.
HERO: If it proves so, then loving goes by haps:
Some Cupid kills with arrows, some with traps.
Exeunt **HERO** *and* **URSULA.**

BEATRICE: (*coming forward*)
What fire is in mine ears? Can this be true?
Stand I condemn'd for pride and scorn so much?
Contempt, farewell! and maiden pride, adieu!
No glory lives behind the back of such.
And, Benedick, love on; I will requite thee,
Taming my wild heart to thy loving hand:
If thou dost love, my kindness shall incite thee
To bind our loves up in a <u>holy band</u>;
For others say thou dost deserve, and I
Believe it better than reportingly.
Exit.

SCENE 2. Don Pedro, Claudio, Leonato and Benedick talk about the Prince's plans for the future. Benedick announces that he has changed and Don Pedro and Claudio realise that he is in love. Benedick leaves with Leonato, probably to discuss his future marriage to Beatrice. The mood changes when Don John tells Don Pedro and Claudio about Hero's 'affair' with Borachio. If what he says is true, Claudio and Don Pedro agree to disgrace her in public at the wedding the next day.

SCENE 3. A street.
Enter **DOGBERRY** *and* **VERGES** *with the Watch.*
DOGBERRY: Are you good men and true?
VERGES: Yea, or else it were pity but they should suffer salvation, body and soul.
DOGBERRY: Nay, that were a punishment too good for them, if they should have any allegiance in them, being chosen for the Prince's <u>watch</u>.
VERGES: Well, give them their charge, neighbour Dogberry.
DOGBERRY: First, who think you the most <u>desertless</u> man to be constable?

To really emphasise what a catch Benedick would be, the two ladies now talk about how well known he is across the country and how impressive his reputation is.

Ursula cleverly, and seamlessly, goes from talking about Benedick to talking about Hero's marriage. Beatrice also begins to think about marriage, as we can see from her next speech.

This soliloquy is very similar to Benedick's in the previous scene. Beatrice's confusion is shown by her use of RHETORICAL QUESTIONS as she tries to make sense of what she has just overheard.

Beatrice decides that she will fall in love with Benedick, who she believes can 'tame' her wild heart. The fact that she is already referring to a 'holy band' means that she has no hesitation in thinking of him as a husband.

This is the first scene which features the Watch. These characters are deliberately played as slapstick comedians. Shakespeare usually created such roles so the audience could have a break from the more serious action and laugh out loud at some of the more stupid acts.

<u>limed:</u> trapped
<u>holy band:</u> marriage and wedding-ring
<u>watch:</u> watchmen, police officers
<u>desertless:</u> undeserving (but he means exactly the opposite)

Part of what makes Dogberry such a funny character is the way that he muddles his words up and says things which do not make sense, even though he is trying to sound very knowledgeable. Although it is difficult to notice some of his slip-ups today, in Tudor times the audience would have found this very amusing.

Dogberry talks about the duties of being a watchman and talks his men through some of the things they have to do. He says that sleeping is important (even though they should be awake and on duty), but says it is important that nothing gets stolen while they are snoozing.

Even though he is supposed to be a policeman, Dogberry's views on the law are very flexible!

favour: appearance
vagrom: scoundrel, vagabond

FIRST WATCHMAN: Hugh Oatcake, sir, or George Seacoal; for they can write and read.

DOGBERRY: Come hither, neighbour Seacoal. God hath blessed you with a good name. To be a well-favoured man is the gift of fortune; but to write and read comes by nature.

SECOND WATCHMAN: Both which, Master Constable –

DOGBERRY: You have; I knew it would be your answer. Well, for your <u>favour</u>, sir, why, give God thanks, and make no boast of it; and for your writing and reading, let that appear when there is no need of such vanity. You are thought here to be the most senseless and fit man for the constable of the watch; therefore bear you the lantern. This is your charge: you shall comprehend all <u>vagrom</u> men; you are to bid any man stand, in the prince's name.

SECOND WATCHMAN: How if 'a will not stand?

DOGBERRY: Why, then, take no note of him, but let him go; and presently call the rest of the watch together and thank God you are rid of a knave.

VERGES: If he will not stand when he is bidden, he is none of the Prince's subjects.

DOGBERRY: True, and they are to meddle with none but the Prince's subjects. You shall also make no noise in the streets; for for the watch to babble and to talk is most tolerable and not to be endured.

WATCHMAN: We will rather sleep than talk; we know what belongs to a watch.

DOGBERRY: Why, you speak like an ancient and most quiet watchman; for I cannot see how sleeping should offend; only, have a care that your bills be not stolen. Well, you are to call at all the ale-houses, and bid those that are drunk get them to bed.

WATCHMAN: How if they will not?

DOGBERRY: Why, then, let them alone till they are sober; if they make you not then the better answer, you may say they are not the men you took them for.

WATCHMAN: Well, sir.

DOGBERRY: If you meet a thief, you may suspect him, by virtue of your office, to be no true man; and, for such kind of men, the less you meddle or make with them, why the more is for your honesty.

WATCHMAN: If we know him to be a thief, shall we not lay hands on him?

DOGBERRY: Truly, by your office, you may; but I think they that touch pitch will be defiled. The most peaceable way for you, if you do take a thief, is to let him show himself what he is and steal out of your company.

VERGES: You have been always called a merciful man, partner.

The comic exchange continues …

46

DOGBERRY: One word more, honest neighbours. I pray you watch about Signior Leonato's door; for the wedding being there to-morrow, there is a great coil tonight. Adieu: be <u>vigitant</u>, I beseech you.
*Exeunt **DOGBERRY** and **VERGES**.*

*Enter **BORACHIO** and **CONRADE**.*
BORACHIO: What Conrade!
WATCHMAN: (*aside*) Peace! stir not.
BORACHIO: Conrade, I say!
CONRADE: Here, man, I am at thy elbow.
BORACHIO: Mass, and my elbow itched; I thought there would a scab follow.
CONRADE: I will owe thee an answer for that; and now forward with thy tale.
BORACHIO: Stand thee close, then, under this pent-house, for it drizzles rain; and I will, like a true drunkard, utter all to thee.
WATCHMAN: (*aside*) Some treason, masters; yet stand close.
BORACHIO: Therefore know I have earned of Don John a thousand <u>ducats</u>.
CONRADE: Is it possible that any villany should be so dear?
BORACHIO: Thou shouldst rather ask if it were possible any villany should be so rich; for when rich villains have need of poor ones, poor ones may make what price they will.
CONRADE: I wonder at it.
BORACHIO: That shows thou art unconfirmed. Thou knowest that the fashion of a doublet, or a hat, or a cloak, is nothing to a man.
CONRADE: Yes, it is apparel.
BORACHIO: I mean, the fashion.
CONRADE: Yes, the fashion is the fashion.
BORACHIO: Tush! I may as well say the fool's the fool. But seest thou not what a deformed thief this fashion is?
WATCHMAN: (*aside*) I know that Deformed; 'a has been a vile thief this seven year; 'a goes up and down like a gentleman. I remember his name.
BORACHIO: Didst thou not hear somebody?
CONRADE: No; 'twas the vane on the house.
BORACHIO: Seest thou not, I say, what a deformed thief this fashion is? How giddily 'a turns about all the hot bloods between fourteen and five-and-thirty? Sometimes fashioning them like Pharaoh's soldiers in the <u>reeky</u> painting, sometime like god Bel's priests in the old church-window, sometime like the shaven Hercules in the smirched worm-eaten tapestry, where his codpiece seems as <u>massy</u> as his club?
CONRADE: All this I see; and I see that the fashion wears out more apparel than the man. But art not thou thyself giddy with the fashion too, that thou hast shifted out of thy tale into telling me of the fashion?

Interestingly, Dogberry is more perceptive here. He tells Verges that because it is the night before Claudio's wedding they should be more vigilant in case there is any trouble. He does not know how right he is!

In a dramatically ironic moment, as soon as Dogberry and Verges leave, Borachio enters. Remember, it was his idea to pretend to have an affair with Hero. He enters in a drunken state, gloating because of the money he has just earned.

Borachio explains what he has just done by talking about fashion and clothes. This emphasises the idea of disguise within the play.

Although the watchmen are not the most reliable police force, they have remained on stage to overhear what Borachio is saying. An aside is when a character talks directly to the audience. In this comment, one watchman explains that he knows Borachio is a bad character and one not to be trusted.

The vile nature of Borachio's character and actions are shown by all the references to filth and rottenness, such as 'reeky', 'worm-eaten' and 'smirched'. His influence has ruined the beautiful and clean reputation of Hero.

<u>vigitant:</u> he means 'vigilant'
<u>ducats:</u> gold and silver coins used at the time
<u>reeky:</u> filthy
<u>massy:</u> huge, massive

To help the audience remember Borachio's plot, he boasts to Conrade about how he made love to Margaret at Hero's window, in front of Claudio, Don John and Don Pedro. He made sure that he used Hero's name so that the onlookers were truly deceived.

Borachio comments that Claudio was furious and that, in his anger, he declared he would shame Hero in front of everyone in the church the next day.

Despite their apparent uselessness, the watchmen realise they have overheard true villainy and arrest Borachio and Conrade for their past actions.

BORACHIO: Not so, neither: but know that I have tonight wooed Margaret, the Lady Hero's gentlewoman, by the name of Hero; she leans me out at her mistress' chamber window, bids me a thousand times good night – I tell this tale vilely – I should first tell thee how the Prince, Claudio and my master, planted and placed and possessed by my master Don John, saw afar off in the orchard this amiable encounter.

CONRADE: And thought they Margaret was Hero?

BORACHIO: Two of them did, the Prince and Claudio; but the devil my master knew she was Margaret; and partly by his oaths, which first possessed them, partly by the dark night, which did deceive them, but chiefly by my villany, which did confirm any slander that Don John had made, away went Claudio enraged; swore he would meet her, as he was appointed, next morning at the temple, and there, before the whole congregation, shame her with what he saw o'er night and send her home again without a husband.

FIRST WATCHMAN: We charge you, in the Prince's name, stand!

SECOND WATCHMAN: Call up the right Master Constable. We have here recovered the most dangerous piece of lechery that ever was known in the commonwealth.

FIRST WATCHMAN: And one Deformed is one of them; I know him; 'a wears a lock.

CONRADE: Masters, masters –

SECOND WATCHMAN: You'll be made bring Deformed forth, I warrant you.

CONRADE: Masters –

FIRST WATCHMAN: Never speak: we charge you let us obey you to go with us.

BORACHIO: We are like to prove a goodly commodity, being taken up of these men's bills.

CONRADE: A commodity in question, I warrant you. Come, we'll obey you.

Exeunt.

SCENE 4. This short scene takes place in Hero's room. She, Ursula and Margaret are discussing what she will wear for her wedding the next day. When Beatrice enters, the women realise she is in love with Benedick but is not quite sure what to do about these new feelings.

SCENE 5. This scene is set in a room in Leonato's house. Dogberry and Verges try to explain about the men they have just arrested, but Leonato finds them so frustrating (they cannot explain themselves properly) that he asks them to leave and give him some privacy before the wedding. The two police officers leave to cross-examine the villains themselves.

ACT 3 QUESTIONS

Understanding the plot
1. Who is involved in the scheme to make Beatrice fall in love with Benedick?
2. How do the ladies begin their conversation about Benedick?
3. In what way does Don John say that Hero has been disloyal?
4. How much did Borachio earn for his part in Don John's plan?
5. Which characters do the nightwatchmen arrest?

Who says this?
1. 'Of this matter is little Cupid's crafty arrow made.'
2. 'Are you sure that Benedick loves Beatrice so entirely?'
3. 'What fire is in mine ears?'
4. 'I have toothache.'
5. 'I will join with thee to disgrace her.'

Name the character
1. Who fetches Beatrice after saying she has overheard a conversation in the garden?
2. Who first informs Claudio of Hero's 'disgrace'?
3. Who tells the watchmen about their duties?
4. Who trims his beard and drenches himself in a herbal aftershave?
5. Who gets frustrated by Dogberry?

Understanding character
1. What makes Beatrice consider her feelings for Benedick?
2. How does Don John make his news more convincing?
3. What is the dramatic purpose of the nightwatchmen?
4. How is the foolish Dogberry also quite careful?
5. Why is Claudio's reaction to the news of Hero's unfaithfulness surprising?

Themes and imagery
1. News and gossip: In what two ways is this theme developed in Act 3?
2. Love: Who realises they are in love in Scene 1?
3. Love: What does Benedick ironically compare being in love to?
4. What is significant about the cold cure 'Carduus Benedictus' that Margaret recommends?
5. What is the significance of Hero's heart being 'heavy' before the wedding?

ACT 4

It is Claudio's and Hero's wedding day and Leonato is very anxious that **FRIAR FRANCIS** should get on with the service as quickly as possible. The ceremony starts, then Claudio insults Hero, publicly calling her a whore, and says that he will not marry her. He explains that he saw her at her window with another man and overheard their conversation in which he learnt that this was one of numerous similar meetings.

 The other characters are all stunned, but Leonato is inclined to believe that what Claudio says might be true. Beatrice and Benedick have faith in Hero, who faints from the stress of it all.

When Claudio, Don Pedro and Don John have left the scene, the Friar, who is sure that Hero is innocent, comes up with a plan. He suggests that she is kept hidden and that the news is announced that she has died from the shock of being accused. This will make Claudio truly value what he has lost and he will regret his actions. Meanwhile, they will try to discover what has led to the accusation. If Hero turns out to be guilty, Leonato can quietly have her placed in a nunnery, where she can remain for the rest of her life. If her innocence is proven, the marriage might still be able to take place. Leonato agrees to this idea and all the characters but Beatrice and Benedick leave to put it into action.

 Benedick tries to comfort Beatrice, who is very upset at the way her cousin has been treated by Claudio. They confess their feelings for each other and Benedick offers to do anything for Beatrice to prove his love. Her reply is to tell him to kill his friend Claudio. He at first refuses to do this, but when Beatrice persists he agrees to challenge him.

The Watch bring their prisoners, Conrade and Borachio, to Dogberry and Verges to be interrogated. The Sexton is there to make a written report and has to keep the interview on course, since Dogberry is incompetent and confused. The watchmen give their evidence and Don John's plot is revealed. The **SEXTON**, who now understands its full significance, gives the news that Don John has fled that morning. He goes to show the full report to Leonato.

KEY TO THEMES

 love

 disguise/appearance versus reality

 nature

 gossip/overhearing

 food

 director's notes

 fighting

 marriage

 clothing

 honour

Leonato is in a great hurry to get the wedding service over quickly and even answers a question on Claudio's behalf. It is an honour to have his daughter well married. Maybe he senses there could be a problem and is keen to have the marriage completed. He is also covering for Claudio's evident bad behaviour.

This is an unexpected outburst from Claudio, showing the strength of his anger that Hero is not pure and innocent, which is what he now believes. His emotion is shown through his repetition of words and use of exclamation marks. Benedick tries to make a joke of it, not realising how serious Claudio is.

This is a long speech, said more calmly (at first) in blank verse. Claudio emphasises the contrast between how things appear and what they are really like. He thinks he has been deliberately conned.

recount: relate in detail
conjoined: joined together in marriage
interjections: interruptions
counterpoise: balance
render: give
semblance: appearance

ACT 4

SCENE 1. A church.

Enter DON PEDRO, DON JOHN, LEONATO, FRIAR FRANCIS, CLAUDIO, BENEDICK, HERO, BEATRICE and ATTENDANTS.

LEONATO: Come, Friar Francis, be brief; only to the plain form of marriage, and you shall <u>recount</u> their particular duties afterwards.

FRIAR FRANCIS: You come hither, my lord, to marry this lady?

CLAUDIO: No.

LEONATO: To be married to her; Friar, you come to marry her.

FRIAR FRANCIS: Lady, you come hither to be married to this Count?

HERO: I do.

FRIAR FRANCIS: If either of you know any inward impediment why you should not be <u>conjoined</u>, I charge you, on your souls, to utter it.

CLAUDIO: Know you any, Hero?

HERO: None, my lord.

FRIAR FRANCIS: Know you any, Count?

LEONATO: I dare make his answer, None.

CLAUDIO: O, what men dare do! What men may do! What men daily do, not knowing what they do!

BENEDICK: How now! <u>Interjections</u>? Why, then, some be of laughing, as, ah, ha, he!

CLAUDIO: Stand thee by, Friar. Father, by your leave:
Will you with free and unconstrained soul
Give me this maid, your daughter?

LEONATO: As freely, son, as God did give her me.

CLAUDIO: And what have I to give you back, whose worth
May <u>counterpoise</u> this rich and precious gift?

DON PEDRO: Nothing, unless you <u>render</u> her again.

CLAUDIO: Sweet Prince, you learn me noble thankfulness.
There, Leonato, take her back again,
Give not this rotten orange to your friend;
She's but the sign and <u>semblance</u> of her honour.
Behold how like a maid she blushes here!
O, what authority and show of truth
Can cunning sin cover itself withal!
Comes not that blood as modest evidence
To witness simple virtue? Would you not swear,
All you that see her, that she were a maid,
By these exterior shows? But she is none;
She knows the heat of a luxurious bed.
Her blush is guiltiness, not modesty.

LEONATO: What do you mean, my lord?

Claudio emphasises that his behaviour to Hero has been totally honourable.

Hero's use of the word 'seem'd' sets Claudio into a fury again, because it reminds him how he has been fooled by her outward appearance. His words turn out to be completely unfair, but if Hero had deceived him and behaved dishonourably, he would at that time have been expected to react like this.

Don Pedro has to support Claudio, not Hero or Leonato, because his reputation and honour are at stake. If his friend is insulted it means an insult to him too, because he arranged the marriage.

Don John does not say much in this scene, but all his words have a purpose. Here, he keeps his evil plan on track with a short statement about fact and truth. Notice how for once Beatrice is lost for words … at the moment.

approved wanton: a person proven to be free with their sexual favours
extenuate: lessen
Dian in her orb: the moon in her orbit (Diana was goddess of the moon)
intemperate: uncontrolled
Venus: goddess of love
stale: prostitute
nuptial: marriage
catechising: asking questions (usually about religious beliefs)
ruffian: a rough person

CLAUDIO: Not to be married,
Not to knit my soul to an **approved wanton**.
LEONATO: Dear my lord, if you, in your own proof,
Have vanquish'd the resistance of her youth,
And made defeat of her virginity –
CLAUDIO: I know what you would say. If I have known her,
You will say she did embrace me as a husband,
And so **extenuate** the 'forehand sin.
No, Leonato,
I never tempted her with word too large,
But, as a brother to his sister, show'd
Bashful sincerity and comely love.
HERO: And seem'd I ever otherwise to you?
CLAUDIO: Out on thee! Seeming! I will write against it.
You seem to me as **Dian in her orb**,
As chaste as is the bud ere it be blown;
But you are more **intemperate** in your blood
Than **Venus**, or those pamper'd animals
That rage in savage sensuality.
HERO: Is my lord well, that he doth speak so wide?
LEONATO: Sweet Prince, why speak not you?
DON PEDRO: What should I speak?
I stand dishonour'd, that have gone about
To link my dear friend to a common **stale**.
LEONATO: Are these things spoken, or do I but dream?
DON JOHN: Sir, they are spoken, and these things are true.
BENEDICK: This looks not like a **nuptial**.
HERO: True? O God!
CLAUDIO: Leonato, stand I here?
Is this the Prince? Is this the Prince's brother?
Is this face Hero's? Are our eyes our own?
LEONATO: All this is so; but what of this, my lord?
CLAUDIO: Let me but move one question to your daughter;
And, by that fatherly and kindly power
That you have in her, bid her answer truly.
LEONATO: I charge thee do so, as thou art my child.
HERO: O God defend me! How am I beset!
What kind of **catechising** call you this?
CLAUDIO: To make you answer truly to your name.
HERO: Is it not Hero? Who can blot that name
With any just reproach?
CLAUDIO: Marry, that can Hero;
Hero itself can blot out Hero's virtue.
What man was he talk'd with you yesternight
Out at your window betwixt twelve and one?
Now, if you are a maid, answer to this.
HERO: I talk'd with no man at that hour, my lord.
DON PEDRO: Why, then are you no maiden. Leonato,
I am sorry you must hear. Upon mine honour,
Myself, my brother and this grieved Count
Did see her, hear her, at that hour last night
Talk with a **ruffian** at her chamber window

Who hath, indeed, most like a liberal villain,
Confess'd the vile encounters they have had
A thousand times in secret.
DON JOHN: <u>Fie</u>, fie! they are not to be named, my lord,
Not to be spoke of;
There is not chastity enough in language
Without offence to utter them. Thus, pretty lady,
I am sorry for thy much misgovernment.
CLAUDIO: O Hero, what a Hero hadst thou been,
If half thy outward graces had been placed
About thy thoughts and counsels of thy heart!
But fare thee well, most foul, most fair! Farewell,
Thou pure <u>impiety</u> and impious purity!
For thee I'll lock up all the gates of love,
And on my eyelids shall <u>conjecture</u> hang,
To turn all beauty into thoughts of harm,
And never shall it more be gracious.
LEONATO: Hath no man's dagger here a point for me?
HERO swoons.
BEATRICE: Why, how now, cousin! Wherefore sink you
  down?
DON JOHN: Come, let us go. These things, come thus to light,
  Smother her spirits up.
Exeunt **DON PEDRO, DON JOHN** *and* **CLAUDIO.**

BENEDICK: How doth the lady?
BEATRICE: Dead, I think. Help, uncle!
Hero! Why, Hero! Uncle! Signior Benedick! Friar!
LEONATO: O Fate! Take not away thy heavy hand.
 Death is the fairest cover for her shame
 That may be wish'd for.
BEATRICE: How now, cousin Hero!
FRIAR FRANCIS: Have comfort, lady.
LEONATO: Dost thou look up?
FRIAR FRANCIS: Yea, wherefore should she not?
LEONATO: Wherefore! Why, doth not every earthly thing
 Cry shame upon her? Could she here deny
 The story that is printed in her blood?
 Do not live, Hero, do not ope thine eyes;
 For, did I think thou wouldst not quickly die,
 Thought I thy spirits were stronger than thy shames,
 Myself would, <u>on the rearward of reproaches</u>,
 Strike at thy life. Grieved I, I had but one?
 Chid I for that at frugal Nature's frame?
 O, one too much by thee! Why had I one?
 Why ever wast thou lovely in my eyes?
 Why had I not with charitable hand
 Took up a beggar's issue at my gates,
 Who <u>smirch'd</u> thus and <u>mired with infamy</u>,
 I might have said 'No part of it is mine;
 This shame derives itself from unknown loins'?
 But mine and mine I loved and mine I praised
 And mine that I was proud on, mine so much

No wonder Don John does not want to give any details of this vast number of 'vile encounters'. There is no evidence at all to back them up, since all are lies.

'Hero' was the name of a girl in legend who was faithful to her lover, so someone called Hero might be expected to show similar qualities. Claudio calls Hero 'most foul, most fair', which sounds at first as though he is contradicting himself. What he means is that Hero looks most lovely but is, in character and behaviour, most dreadful. Although he is emotional he seems to have carefully planned this speech, because he uses language cleverly again in the next line.

Hero faints after her father's words, which seem the final straw for her because he is not taking her side. He presumes she is guilty, whereas Beatrice, Benedick and the Friar support her.

Don John makes a hurried exit before there is a chance of discovering his wicked plot. We do not see him again.

To a modern audience, Leonato appears very heartless here, but if his daughter has dishonoured the family name, death would be seen as preferable to living in shame.

<u>fie:</u> an exclamation expressing disgust
<u>impiety:</u> a lack of respect or dutifulness
<u>conjecture:</u> doubt, suspicion
<u>on the rearward of reproaches:</u> after these shames
<u>smirch'd:</u> dirtied, dishonoured
<u>mired with infamy:</u> tainted with bad reputation

Leonato repeats personal pronouns, particularly 'mine' (which stands here for Hero). He is very aware of the hurt to himself, both personal and public, caused by Hero's disgrace. He valued her so highly that she has further to fall. He uses a vivid image of falling into black ink to show how stained her character now is.

It is rare that Benedick is lost for words, which shows how shocked and upset he is. From this point onwards we see a more serious, less shallow side to him.

The Friar reacts reasonably and unemotionally in comparison to Leonato. He realises that it is highly likely that Hero is innocent. He looks at her appearance and sees the truth.

Leonato seems determined to think badly of Hero.

Hero protests her innocence, which makes the Friar and Benedick more certain that there is some misunderstanding. Benedick immediately suspects Don John.

belied: lied about

tenor: theme

biting: bitter

perjury: deliberately giving false
information while under oath

unmeet: unsuitable

misprision: mistake, misunderstanding

That I myself was to myself not mine,
Valuing of her – why, she, O, she is fallen
Into a pit of ink, that the wide sea
Hath drops too few to wash her clean again
And salt too little which may season give
To her foul-tainted flesh!
BENEDICK: Sir, sir, be patient.
For my part, I am so attired in wonder,
I know not what to say.
BEATRICE: O, on my soul, my cousin is **belied**!
BENEDICK: Lady, were you her bedfellow last night?
BEATRICE: No, truly not; although, until last night,
I have this twelvemonth been her bedfellow.
LEONATO: Confirm'd, confirm'd! O, that is stronger made
Which was before barr'd up with ribs of iron!
Would the two Princes lie, and Claudio lie,
Who loved her so, that, speaking of her foulness,
Wash'd it with tears? Hence from her, let her die!
FRIAR FRANCIS: Hear me a little;
For I have only been silent so long
And given way unto this course of fortune
By noting of the lady. I have mark'd
A thousand blushing apparitions
To start into her face, a thousand innocent shames
In angel whiteness beat away those blushes;
And in her eye there hath appear'd a fire,
To burn the errors that these Princes hold
Against her maiden truth. Call me a fool;
Trust not my reading nor my observations,
Which with experimental seal doth warrant
The **tenor** of my book; trust not my age,
My reverence, calling, nor divinity,
If this sweet lady lie not guiltless here
Under some **biting** error.
LEONATO: Friar, it cannot be.
Thou seest that all the grace that she hath left
Is that she will not add to her damnation
A sin of **perjury**; she not denies it:
Why seek'st thou then to cover with excuse
That which appears in proper nakedness?
FRIAR FRANCIS: Lady, what man is he you are
accused of?
HERO: They know that do accuse me; I know none.
If I know more of any man alive
Than that which maiden modesty doth warrant,
Let all my sins lack mercy! O my father,
Prove you that any man with me conversed
At hours **unmeet**, or that I yesternight
Maintain'd the change of words with any creature,
Refuse me, hate me, torture me to death!
FRIAR FRANCIS: There is some strange **misprision** in
the Princes.

BENEDICK: Two of them have the very **bent** of honour;
And if their wisdoms be misled in this,
The practise of it lives in John the bastard,
Whose spirits toil in frame of villanies.
LEONATO: I know not. If they speak but truth of her,
These hands shall tear her; if they wrong her honour,
The proudest of them shall well hear of it.
Time hath not yet so dried this blood of mine,
Nor age so eat up my invention,
Nor fortune made such havoc of my means,
Nor my bad life **reft** me so much of friends,
But they shall find, awaked in such a kind,
Both strength of limb and policy of mind,
Ability in means and choice of friends,
To quit me of them throughly.
FRIAR FRANCIS: Pause awhile,
And let my counsel sway you in this case.
Your daughter here the Princes left for dead:
Let her awhile be secretly kept in,
And publish it that she is dead indeed.
Maintain a mourning ostentation,
And on your family's old monument
Hang mournful epitaphs and do all rites
That appertain unto a burial.
LEONATO: What shall become of this? What will this do?
FRIAR FRANCIS: Marry, this well carried shall on her behalf
Change slander to remorse; that is some good.
But not for that dream I on this strange course,
But on this **travail** look for greater birth.
She dying, as it must so be maintain'd,
Upon the instant that she was accused,
Shall be lamented, pitied and excused
Of every hearer; for it so falls out
That what we have we prize not to the worth
Whiles we enjoy it, but being lack'd and lost,
Why, then we rack the value, then we find
The virtue that possession would not show us
Whiles it was ours. So will it fare with Claudio.
When he shall hear she died upon his words,
The idea of her life shall sweetly creep
Into his study of imagination,
And every lovely organ of her life
Shall come **apparell'd** in more precious habit,
More moving, delicate and full of life,
Into the eye and prospect of his soul,
Than when she lived indeed. Then shall he mourn,
If ever love had interest in his liver,
And wish he had not so accused her –
No, though he thought his accusation true.
Let this be so, and doubt not but success
Will fashion the event in better shape
Than I can lay it down in likelihood.
But if all aim but this be levell'd false,

At last, Leonato is admitting the possibility that his daughter may be innocent.

The Friar has a cunning plan. In Shakespeare's plays Friars have a habit of devising complex schemes, as Friar Laurence does in *Romeo and Juliet*. They are seen as trustworthy so their advice is taken.

The Friar plans to teach Claudio a lesson by pretending that Hero is dead. This will make Claudio realise what he has lost and has not truly valued. The plan is a combination of two proverbs: 'you don't know what you have until it's gone' and 'absence makes the heart grow fonder'.

bent: full extent (of honour)
reft: deprived
travail: work, plan
apparell'd: dressed
if ever love had interest in his liver: the liver was thought to be the organ where love originated

55

If Hero is not proved to be innocent, she will be hidden away for the rest of her life, perhaps in a nunnery. This would be the only honourable course of action at that time, for no one else would want to marry her and it would be a disgrace to her family to have her living at home.

Notice how Friar Francis now speaks in alternate rhyming lines, which is a change from blank verse. It indicates the end of an episode, and all the characters but Beatrice and Benedick leave the stage. Their relationship is about to change.

Both characters speak in short lines instead of their usual joking and word play. The serious tone is appropriate, since they are about to declare their love for each other. They are both surprised by their feelings.

A lot of Beatrice's language involves eating. Remember that in Act 1 Scene 1 she joked that she promised to eat all that Benedick kills.

At last, Beatrice and Benedick admit their love for each other. It has been obvious to everyone else right from the first scene that they are very attracted to one another.

infamy: scandalous reputation
inwardness: deepest feelings
twine: thread
presently: at once

The supposition of the lady's death
Will quench the wonder of her **infamy**;
And if it sort not well, you may conceal her,
As best befits her wounded reputation,
In some reclusive and religious life,
Out of all eyes, tongues, minds and injuries.
BENEDICK: Signior Leonato, let the Friar advise you:
And though you know my **inwardness** and love
Is very much unto the Prince and Claudio,
Yet, by mine honour, I will deal in this
As secretly and justly as your soul
Should with your body.
LEONATO: Being that I flow in grief,
The smallest **twine** may lead me.
FRIAR FRANCIS: 'Tis well consented. **Presently** away;
For to strange sores strangely they strain the cure.
Come, lady, die to live; this wedding-day
Perhaps is but prolong'd; have patience and endure.
Exeunt all but BENEDICK *and* BEATRICE.

BENEDICK: Lady Beatrice, have you wept all this while?
BEATRICE: Yea, and I will weep a while longer.
BENEDICK: I will not desire that.
BEATRICE: You have no reason; I do it freely.
BENEDICK: Surely I do believe your fair cousin is wronged.
BEATRICE: Ah, how much might the man deserve of me that would right her!
BENEDICK: Is there any way to show such friendship?
BEATRICE: A very even way, but no such friend.
BENEDICK: May a man do it?
BEATRICE: It is a man's office, but not yours.
BENEDICK: I do love nothing in the world so well as you; is not that strange?
BEATRICE: As strange as the thing I know not. It were as possible for me to say I loved nothing so well as you; but believe me not, and yet I lie not; I confess nothing, nor I deny nothing. I am sorry for my cousin.
BENEDICK: By my sword, Beatrice, thou lovest me.
BEATRICE: Do not swear, and eat it.
BENEDICK: I will swear by it that you love me; and I will make him eat it that says I love not you.
BEATRICE: Will you not eat your word?
BENEDICK: With no sauce that can be devised to it. I protest I love thee.
BEATRICE: Why, then, God forgive me!
BENEDICK: What offence, sweet Beatrice?
BEATRICE: You have stayed me in a happy hour; I was about to protest I loved you.
BENEDICK: And do it with all thy heart.
BEATRICE: I love you with so much of my heart that none is left to protest.
BENEDICK: Come, bid me do any thing for thee.

BEATRICE: Kill Claudio.
BENEDICK: Ha! Not for the wide world.
BEATRICE: You kill me to deny it. Farewell.
BENEDICK: Tarry, sweet Beatrice.
BEATRICE: I am gone though I am here; there is no love in you. Nay, I pray you, let me go.
BENEDICK: Beatrice –
BEATRICE: In faith, I will go.
BENEDICK: We'll be friends first.
BEATRICE: You dare easier be friends with me than fight with mine enemy.
BENEDICK: Is Claudio thine enemy?
BEATRICE: Is he not **approved** in the height a villain that hath slandered, scorned, dishonoured my kinswoman? O that I were a man! What, **bear her in hand** until they come to take hands, and then, with public accusation, uncovered slander, **unmitigated rancour** – O God, that I were a man! I would eat his heart in the market-place.
BENEDICK: Hear me, Beatrice –
BEATRICE: Talk with a man out at a window! A **proper** saying!
BENEDICK: Nay, but, Beatrice –
BEATRICE: Sweet Hero! She is wronged, she is slandered, she is undone.
BENEDICK: Beat –
BEATRICE: Princes and counties! Surely, a princely testimony, a goodly count, **Count Comfect**; a sweet gallant, surely! O that I were a man for his sake! or that I had any friend would be a man for my sake! But manhood is melted into curtsies, valour into compliment, and men are only turned into tongue, and trim ones too. He is now as valiant as **Hercules** that only tells a lie and swears it. I cannot be a man with wishing, therefore I will die a woman with grieving.
BENEDICK: Tarry, good Beatrice. By this hand, I love thee.
BEATRICE: Use it for my love some other way than swearing by it.
BENEDICK: Think you in your soul the Count Claudio hath wronged Hero?
BEATRICE: Yea, as sure as I have a thought or a soul.
BENEDICK: Enough, I am engaged; I will challenge him. I will kiss your hand, and so I leave you. By this hand, Claudio shall render me a dear account. As you hear of me, so think of me. Go, comfort your cousin; I must say she is dead; and so, farewell.
Exeunt.

This is a shocking and completely unexpected answer that changes the mood of the scene. Beatrice is not joking, but she is speaking impulsively because she is so upset about the treatment of her cousin. She sees this request to kill Claudio as a test of Benedick's love for her.

Beatrice becomes increasingly angry as she talks about Claudio's actions. She wishes that she was a man, so she could challenge Claudio herself, or that she could find a man who was brave in action as well as in speech to act on her behalf.

At the end of the scene Benedick agrees to fight a duel with Claudio. This could be very serious, but since the play is a comedy the audience can be sure that things will be resolved without a fight to the death.

approved: proved
bear her in hand: lead her falsely on
unmitigated rancour: pouring out spite and ill will without letting up
proper: true, worthy (she is being sarcastic)
Count Comfect: Count Lollipop (i.e. sweets)
Hercules: a Greek hero

This is the first we hear of what has become of Don John. It is now clear that all the muddles can be sorted out, because the real villain has been unmasked. At least someone sensible is going to Leonato's with all the news!

Dogberry has to have the last word – at great length! Even though the Sexton has left on important business, he wants him there to record the insults that he thinks he has received from Conrade. In fact, Conrade has summed him up perfectly by calling him an 'ass', though Dogberry is too full of his own importance to realise this. He returns to this theme in Act 5. Dogberry lists everything that he thinks makes him an admirable person, including the fact that he owns not one, but 'two gowns' – perhaps the outer garments he wears on official business.

SCENE 2 takes place in a prison, where Dogberry and Verges try to question Conrade and Borachio. They have no idea how to go about  *it and have to be helped by the Sexton, whose job is to provide a written report of events. Eventually the crime is explained. We join the scene in the last half, after the villains have provided a full confession.*

DOGBERRY: O villain! thou wilt be condemned into everlasting <u>redemption</u> for this.
SEXTON: What else?
WATCHMAN: This is all.
SEXTON: And this is more, masters, than you can deny. Prince John is this morning secretly stolen away; Hero was in this manner accused, in this very manner refused, and upon the grief of this suddenly died. Master Constable, let these men be bound, and brought to Leonato's: I will go before and show him their examination.
Exit.

DOGBERRY: Come, let them be <u>opinioned</u>.
VERGES: Let them be in the hands –
CONRADE: Off, <u>coxcomb</u>!
DOGBERRY: God's my life, where's the Sexton? Let him write down the Prince's officer coxcomb. Come, bind them. Thou naughty <u>varlet</u>!
CONRADE: Away! you are an ass, you are an ass.
DOGBERRY: Dost thou not <u>suspect</u> my place? Dost thou not suspect my years? O that he were here to write me down an ass! But, masters, remember that I am an ass; though it be not written down, yet forget not that I am an ass. No, thou villain, thou art full of <u>piety</u>, as shall be proved upon thee by good witness. I am a wise fellow, and, which is more, an officer, and, which is more, a householder, and, which is more, as pretty a piece of flesh as any is in Messina, and one that knows the law, go to; and a rich fellow enough, go to; and a fellow that hath had losses, and one that hath two gowns and every thing handsome about him. Bring him away. O that I had been writ down an ass!
Exeunt.

<u>redemption:</u> this means being 'saved from sin' but Dogberry intends the opposite – 'damnation'

<u>opinioned:</u> he means 'pinioned', i.e. tied up

<u>coxcomb:</u> a silly, vain man; in modern terms we might say he has ideas above his station

<u>varlet:</u> rascal

<u>suspect:</u> he means 'respect'

<u>piety:</u> this means 'goodness' and 'holiness', whereas Dogberry really means 'evil'

Understanding the plot

1. What reason does Claudio give for refusing to marry Hero?
2. Hero faints just before Claudio leaves. What news of her will be given to him?
3. Where would Hero go, if she were proven guilty?
4. Who has received a thousand ducats payment?
5. What news is given of Don John?

Who says this?

1. 'Her blush is guiltiness, not modesty.'
2. 'Death is the fairest cover for her shame.'
3. 'I do love nothing in the world so well as you.'
4. 'Kill Claudio.'
5. 'O that I had been writ down an ass!'

Name the character

1. Who asks the Friar to go through the marriage ceremony quickly?
2. Who backs up Claudio in his accusations of Hero?
3. Who devises a plan to help Hero?
4. Who tries to interrogate Conrade and Borachio?
5. Who goes to tell Leonato the truth about the scheme to dishonour Hero?

Understanding character

1. Which side of Benedick's character do we mostly see in this Act, the serious or the joking?
2. Why does Hero faint when Claudio accuses her?
3. Why does Leonato believe Claudio and Don Pedro?
4. Who does Beatrice turn to for help, when her cousin is wronged?
5. Which word best sums up Dogberry: modest/self-important/generous/impatient?

Themes and imagery

1. Who is compared to a 'rotten orange'?
2. Love: Which two characters contribute to the theme of love?
3. Dishonour: Who has 'fallen / Into a pit of ink'?
4. Appearance/reality: Find one example of the theme of appearance/reality from Scene 1.
5. Who is referred to as 'Count Comfect'?

ACT 5

Antonio advises Leonato that he is harming himself by continuing with his grief and anger. Leonato rejects his brother's words, because he thinks that only someone who has been in a similar situation can understand. Although he has not yet heard the evidence of the Sexton, Leonato has come to believe that Hero has been falsely accused by Claudio and Don Pedro and that they must be made to realise this. When they arrive he treats them coldly and angrily and is prepared to fight to prove that Claudio has acted wrongly. Antonio, who has been the calmer of the two brothers, now talks aggressively and has to be restrained by Leonato. Don Pedro expresses regret that Hero has died, but insists that she is guilty.

After Leonato and Antonio leave, Benedick arrives. He does not join in with his friends' jokes, and challenges Claudio to a duel. As he leaves he tells Don Pedro that Don John has fled. Don Pedro and Claudio are forced to recognise the seriousness of their position when Dogberry, Verges and the Watch appear with their prisoners, Conrade and Borachio. They learn the full details of Don John's plot.

Leonato has also now been told the truth by the Sexton. Claudio and Don Pedro are deeply apologetic and offer to do anything to make up for their actions. Leonato asks them to make public Hero's innocence and to visit her tomb that night, bringing with them a verse praising her memory. He also requests that Claudio should marry Antonio's 'daughter' the very next day. Claudio agrees to all of these conditions, even though he has never seen Antonio's daughter. Leonato presumes that Margaret was also involved in Don John's scheming, but Borachio makes it clear that she had no idea of what was going on.

Benedick asks Margaret to help him to see Beatrice. While he is waiting for her to arrive, he tries to write a verse in praise of her, but he realises this is not a method of wooing suited to him. Benedick wants to talk about love, but Beatrice first wants to know what has happened between him and Claudio. They have a brief conversation about their feelings, but are interrupted by Ursula who calls them back to the house where everything is in chaos because of the revelations about Don John's plot.

Claudio, Don Pedro and musicians go to Hero's tomb to deliver her epitaph and a song. Claudio says he will make this a yearly ritual.

All Leonato's household are gathered for the wedding. Benedick asks the Friar to conduct a marriage for him and tells Leonato that he and Beatrice love each other. Claudio is still determined to marry Antonio's daughter, whatever she may be like, so Antonio brings in all the ladies, who are wearing masks. When Hero removes her mask, Claudio and Don Pedro react with delight and amazement. Leonato explains that she only 'died' while the dishonour against her persisted.

Beatrice and Benedick agree to marry and Benedick restores his friendship with Claudio. The news comes that Don John has been captured and brought back to Messina. The play ends with music and dancing.

KEY TO THEMES

 love

 disguise/appearance versus reality

 nature

 gossip/overhearing

 food

 director's notes

 fighting

 marriage

 clothing

 honour

Remember that Antonio and Leonato still do not know that Hero has been proved innocent. Leonato is taking the situation very badly and is deeply depressed. Antonio is trying to help him, without success.

This is a long speech from Leonato. To keep the audience interested, the actor would need to emphasise Leonato's desperate, emotional state. He might also pace about the stage. Antonio, who says very little, would be looking concerned.

Leonato says that only someone who has gone through a similar experience to himself can possibly understand how it feels. The marked part of this speech is all one long sentence, which shows just how worked up he is and how involved he is in his sorrow.

SCENE 1. *Before* LEONATO's *house.*

Enter LEONATO *and* ANTONIO.

ANTONIO: If you go on thus, you will kill yourself:
And 'tis not wisdom thus to **second** grief
Against yourself.

LEONATO:　　　　I pray thee, cease thy counsel,
Which falls into mine ears as profitless
As water in a sieve. Give not me counsel,
Nor let no comforter delight mine ear
But such a one whose wrongs do suit with mine.
Bring me a father that so loved his child,
Whose joy of her is overwhelm'd like mine,
And bid him speak of patience;
Measure his woe the length and breadth of mine
And let it answer every strain for strain,
As thus for thus and such a grief for such,
In every **lineament**, branch, shape, and form;
If such a one will smile and stroke his beard,
And sorrow wag, cry 'hem!' when he should groan,
Patch grief with proverbs, make misfortune drunk
With **candle-wasters** – bring him yet to me,
And I of him will gather patience.
But there is no such man; for, brother, men
Can counsel and speak comfort to that grief
Which they themselves not feel; but, tasting it,
Their counsel turns to passion, which before
Would give **preceptial medicine to rage**,
Fetter strong madness in a silken thread,
Charm ache with air and agony with words.
No, no; 'tis all men's office to speak patience
To those that wring under the load of sorrow,
But no man's virtue nor sufficiency
To be so moral when he shall endure
The like himself. Therefore give me no counsel;
My griefs cry louder than advertisement.

ANTONIO: Therein do men from children nothing differ.

LEONATO: I pray thee, peace. I will be flesh and blood;
For there was never yet philosopher
That could endure the toothache patiently,
However they have writ the style of gods
And made a push at chance and sufferance.

ANTONIO: Yet bend not all the harm upon yourself;
Make those that do offend you suffer too.

LEONATO: There thou speak'st reason; nay, I will do so.
My soul doth tell me Hero is belied;
And that shall Claudio know; so shall the Prince,
And all of them that thus dishonour her.

ANTONIO: Here comes the Prince and Claudio hastily.

Enter DON PEDRO *and* CLAUDIO.

second: support; when you fight a duel, a friend acts as your supporter or 'second', but takes no part in the fighting
lineament: line or contour
patch: mend
candle-wasters: hard-working students
preceptial medicine to rage: particular rules to cure being so upset
fetter: chain up

Don Pedro and Claudio are polite but keen to leave. Leonato immediately attacks them with words. Later, he talks about fighting a duel with Claudio.

In this part of the scene there is a lot of emphasis on the age of Leonato. As a result, the audience are more impressed with the fact that he is prepared to fight in an honourable cause.

Leonato completely mistrusts Claudio and thinks that he is being mocked. Since both he and his daughter have been publicly humiliated and dishonoured, he has no choice but to challenge the much younger man. Remember that although he now calls his daughter 'innocent', he was very recently all too ready to believe the worst of her.

Claudio refuses the challenge and tries to calm things down. This makes Leonato and Antonio even more angry and determined to fight. Remember that Hero is not dead, although she has been wronged, so they are putting on quite a convincing act!

dissembler: deceiver

beshrew: curse

fleer: mock

dotard: doddery old man

nice fence: graceful fencing

daff: push away

foining: thrusting

apes, braggarts, Jacks, milksops: fools, boasters, immoral lads, cowards

DON PEDRO: Good den, good den.

CLAUDIO: Good day to both of you.

LEONATO: Hear you, my lords!

DON PEDRO: We have some haste, Leonato.

LEONATO: Some haste, my lord! Well, fare you well, my lord;
Are you so hasty now? Well, all is one.

DON PEDRO: Nay, do not quarrel with us, good old man.

ANTONIO: If he could right himself with quarreling,
Some of us would lie low.

CLAUDIO: Who wrongs him?

LEONATO: Marry, thou dost wrong me; thou **dissembler**, thou!
Nay, never lay thy hand upon thy sword;
I fear thee not.

CLAUDIO: Marry, **beshrew** my hand,
If it should give your age such cause of fear:
In faith, my hand meant nothing to my sword.

LEONATO: Tush, tush, man; never **fleer** and jest at me;
I speak not like a **dotard** nor a fool,
As under privilege of age to brag
What I have done being young, or what would do
Were I not old. Know, Claudio, to thy head,
Thou hast so wrong'd mine innocent child and me
That I am forced to lay my reverence by
And, with grey hairs and bruise of many days,
Do challenge thee to trial of a man.
I say thou hast belied mine innocent child;
Thy slander hath gone through and through her heart,
And she lies buried with her ancestors –
O, in a tomb where never scandal slept,
Save this of hers, framed by thy villany!

CLAUDIO: My villany?

LEONATO: Thine, Claudio; thine, I say.

DON PEDRO: You say not right, old man.

LEONATO: My lord, my lord,
I'll prove it on his body, if he dare,
Despite his **nice fence** and his active practice,
His May of youth and bloom of lustihood.

CLAUDIO: Away! I will not have to do with you.

LEONATO: Canst thou so **daff** me? Thou hast kill'd my child;
If thou kill'st me, boy, thou shalt kill a man.

ANTONIO: He shall kill two of us, and men indeed;
But that's no matter; let him kill one first.
Win me and wear me; let him answer me.
Come, follow me, boy; come, sir boy, come, follow me;
Sir boy, I'll whip you from your **foining** fence;
Nay, as I am a gentleman, I will.

LEONATO: Brother –

ANTONIO: Content yourself. God knows I loved my niece;
And she is dead, slander'd to death by villains,
That dare as well answer a man indeed
As I dare take a serpent by the tongue.
Boys, **apes, braggarts, Jacks, milksops**!

62

LEONATO: Brother Antony –
ANTONIO: Hold you content. What, man! I know them, yea,
   And what they weigh, even to the utmost scruple –
   Scrambling, out-facing, **fashion-monging** boys,
   That lie and **cog and flout**, deprave and slander,
   Go **anticly**, show outward hideousness,
   And speak off half a dozen dangerous words,
   How they might hurt their enemies, if they durst;
   And this is all.
LEONATO: But, brother Antony –
ANTONIO: Come, 'tis no matter;
   Do not you meddle; let me deal in this.
DON PEDRO: Gentlemen both, we will not wake your
   patience.
   My heart is sorry for your daughter's death,
   But, on my honour, she was charged with nothing
   But what was true and very full of proof.
LEONATO: My lord, my lord –
DON PEDRO: I will not hear you.
LEONATO: No?
   Come, brother; away! I will be heard.
ANTONIO: And shall, or some of us will smart for it.
Exeunt LEONATO and ANTONIO.

DON PEDRO: See, see; here comes the man we went to
   seek.
Enter BENEDICK.
CLAUDIO: Now, signior, what news?
BENEDICK: Good day, my lord.
DON PEDRO: Welcome, signior; you are almost come to
   part almost a **fray**.
CLAUDIO: We had like to have had our two noses snapped
   off with two old men without teeth.
DON PEDRO: Leonato and his brother. What thinkest thou?
   Had we fought, I doubt we should have been too young
   for them.
BENEDICK: In a false quarrel there is no true valour. I
   came to seek you both.
CLAUDIO: We have been up and down to seek thee; for we
   are high-proof melancholy and would fain have it beaten
   away. Wilt thou use thy wit?
BENEDICK: It is in my scabbard; shall I draw it?
DON PEDRO: Dost thou wear thy wit by thy side?
CLAUDIO: Never any did so, though very many have been
   beside their wit. I will bid thee draw, as we do the
   minstrels – draw, to pleasure us.
DON PEDRO: As I am an honest man, he looks pale. Art
   thou sick, or angry?
CLAUDIO: What, courage, man! What though care killed a
   cat, thou hast **mettle** enough in thee to kill care.
BENEDICK: Sir, I shall meet your wit in the career, an you
   charge it against me. I pray you choose another subject.

Now it is Antonio who has become the more worked up, and Leonato who tries to calm him down. He very convincingly acts the part of the grieving uncle, but he has genuine anger against Claudio.

Why does Leonato leave here when he still hasn't won his battle with Don Pedro and Claudio? Perhaps he intends to return with his sword. It also gives Shakespeare a chance to vary the scene by bringing Benedick in.

As soon as Benedick comes in, Don Pedro and Claudio begin joking and show little respect for the two old men who have just left. The audience would be very aware of this, knowing how Hero has been wronged.

His friends are very pleased to see him, but this time Benedick is in no mood for joking.

Don Pedro and Claudio expect Benedick to join in with the joking as he usually does. They do not understand that his mood is really serious. Remember that he has come straight from Beatrice asking him to 'Kill Claudio'.

fashion-monging: fashion-changing
cog and flout: cheat and mock
anticly: grotesquely
fray: fight
mettle: courage

Note the change of mood. Watch the Kenneth Branagh film to see how effectively this part of the scene can be acted.

This speech is said aside, so Don Pedro is not aware of what is taking place, although the audience can hear everything. Claudio accepts the challenge to fight a duel and then jokes to Don Pedro, who seems to think they are talking about a feast, so he does not suspect what has been said. Benedick finds these jokes feeble and out of place.

Don Pedro talks about Beatrice, hoping to draw Benedick into his usual joking mood. This does not work, as you can see, because Benedick does not join in at all. It seems pretty thoughtless and small-minded of Claudio to carry on as if nothing has happened, when he knows how angry Benedick is.

Here Benedick is forced to break his friendship with Don Pedro because of his quarrel with Claudio. He gives him two startling pieces of news: that Don John has disappeared, and that he has challenged Claudio. Calling Claudio 'Lord Lackbeard' reminds us of Beatrice's name for him, which also uses ALLITERATION: 'Count Comfect'.

to turn his girdle: how to put up with it

capon: a castrated cockerel (people still eat these today sometimes)

the tongues: gift for languages

forswore: denied

trans-shape: distort

Lord Lackbeard: an insulting name for Claudio, implying that he is not courageous and manly

CLAUDIO: Nay, then, give him another staff; this last was broke cross.

DON PEDRO: By this light, he changes more and more; I think he be angry indeed.

CLAUDIO: If he be, he knows how <u>to turn his girdle</u>.

BENEDICK: Shall I speak a word in your ear?

CLAUDIO: God bless me from a challenge!

BENEDICK: (*aside to* **CLAUDIO**) You are a villain; I jest not. I will make it good how you dare, with what you dare, and when you dare. Do me right, or I will protest your cowardice. You have killed a sweet lady, and her death shall fall heavy on you. Let me hear from you.

CLAUDIO: Well, I will meet you, so I may have good cheer.

DON PEDRO: What, a feast, a feast?

CLAUDIO: I' faith, I thank him; he hath bid me to a calf's head and a <u>capon</u>; the which if I do not carve most curiously, say my knife's naught. Shall I not find a woodcock too?

BENEDICK: Sir, your wit ambles well; it goes easily.

DON PEDRO: I'll tell thee how Beatrice praised thy wit the other day. I said, thou hadst a fine wit: 'True,' said she, 'a fine little one.' 'No,' said I, 'a great wit.' 'Right,' says she, 'a great gross one.' 'Nay,' said I, 'a good wit.' 'Just,' said she, 'it hurts nobody.' 'Nay,' said I, 'the gentleman is wise.' 'Certain,' said she, 'a wise gentleman.' 'Nay,' said I, 'he hath <u>the tongues</u>.' 'That I believe,' said she, 'for he swore a thing to me on Monday night, which he <u>forswore</u> on Tuesday morning. There's a double tongue; there's two tongues.' Thus did she, an hour together, <u>trans-shape</u> thy particular virtues; yet at last she concluded with a sigh, thou wast the properest man in Italy.

CLAUDIO: For the which she wept heartily, and said she cared not.

DON PEDRO: Yea, that she did; but yet, for all that, an if she did not hate him deadly, she would love him dearly. The old man's daughter told us all.

CLAUDIO: All, all; and, moreover, God saw him when he was hid in the garden.

DON PEDRO: But when shall we set the savage bull's horns on the sensible Benedick's head?

CLAUDIO: Yea, and text underneath, 'Here dwells Benedick the married man'?

BENEDICK: Fare you well, boy; you know my mind. I will leave you now to your gossip-like humour; you break jests as braggarts do their blades, which, God be thanked, hurt not. My lord, for your many courtesies I thank you; I must discontinue your company. Your brother the bastard is fled from Messina. You have among you killed a sweet and innocent lady. For my <u>Lord Lackbeard</u> there, he and I shall meet; and, till then, peace be with him.

Exit.

DON PEDRO: He is in earnest.

CLAUDIO: In most profound earnest; and, I'll warrant you, for the love of Beatrice.

DON PEDRO: And hath challenged thee.

CLAUDIO: Most sincerely.

DON PEDRO: What a pretty thing man is when he goes in his doublet and hose and leaves off his wit!

CLAUDIO: He is then a giant to an ape; but then is an ape a doctor to such a man.

DON PEDRO: But, <u>soft you</u>, let me be; pluck up, my heart, and be <u>sad</u>. Did he not say, my brother was fled?

Enter **DOGBERRY**, **VERGES** *and the Watch with* **CONRADE** *and* **BORACHIO**.

DOGBERRY: Come you, sir; if justice cannot tame you, she shall ne'er weigh more reasons in her balance. Nay, an you be a cursing hypocrite once, you must be looked to.

DON PEDRO: How now? Two of my brother's men bound! Borachio one!

CLAUDIO: <u>Hearken</u> after their offence, my lord.

DON PEDRO: Officers, what offence have these men done?

DOGBERRY: Marry, sir, they have committed false report; moreover, they have spoken untruths; secondarily, they are slanders; sixth and lastly, they have belied a lady; thirdly, they have verified unjust things; and, to conclude, they are lying knaves.

DON PEDRO: First, I ask thee what they have done; thirdly, I ask thee what's their offence; sixth and lastly, why they are committed; and, to conclude, what you lay to their charge.

CLAUDIO: Rightly reasoned, and in his own division; and, by my troth, there's one meaning well suited.

DON PEDRO: Who have you offended, masters, that you are thus bound to your answer? This learned Constable is too cunning to be understood; what's your offence?

BORACHIO: Sweet Prince, let me go no farther to mine answer; do you hear me, and let this Count kill me. I have deceived even your very eyes: what your wisdoms could not discover, these shallow fools have brought to light; who in the night overheard me confessing to this man how Don John your brother <u>incensed me</u> to slander the Lady Hero; how you were brought into the orchard and saw me court Margaret in Hero's garments; how you disgraced her, when you should marry her. My villany they have upon record, which I had rather seal with my death than repeat over to my shame. The lady is dead upon mine and my master's false accusation; and, briefly, I desire nothing but the reward of a villain.

DON PEDRO: Runs not this speech like iron through your blood?

CLAUDIO: I have drunk poison whiles he utter'd it.

DON PEDRO: But did my brother set thee on to this?

Claudio tells Don Pedro that Benedick is behaving in this serious way because of his love for Beatrice. He is more right than he imagines, since it was Beatrice who demanded that Benedick take action against Claudio.

For much of this scene, Don Pedro and Claudio stay on stage while various other characters enter and exit. This helps the audience to see clearly their different changes of mood, particularly when the dreadful truth about their actions towards Hero is at last revealed to them.

Here Dogberry repeats exactly the same piece of information about the crime in different ways. He uses words like 'secondarily' to make his report sound official and important, but he gets the order of his numbers entirely confused. Don Pedro pokes fun at this in his reply.

Details of the crime are briefly given, both for Don Pedro's benefit and as a reminder to the audience. Borachio is sorry for his crime and accepts any punishment he may be given. This is also how Claudio reacts later in the scene.

The strong images of iron and poison used by Don Pedro and Claudio show how devastated they are by Borachio's confession. Don Pedro continues to use strong terms to describe his wicked brother.

<u>soft you</u>: be quiet
<u>sad</u>: serious
<u>hearken</u>: ask
<u>incensed me</u>: put me up

At last Leonato knows the whole truth, which has been explained to him when he was off stage. He refuses to blame Borachio and Don John alone and speaks sarcastically of Don Pedro's and Claudio's 'brave' actions. Obviously Claudio is going to have to prove he is worthy of Hero before he is allowed to marry her. In myths and fables the young hero often had to carry out tasks before winning the girl.

Claudio's first task at the grave will prove that he is properly respectful to the 'dead' Hero. Secondly, he must agree to marry her 'cousin' before setting eyes on her. These two actions will satisfy Leonato's honour.

To a modern audience it might seem strange that Claudio does not ask any questions about this daughter, and does not seem surprised about her existence. In Shakespeare's comedies you just have to accept things which drive the plot forward, no matter how unlikely they may seem.

framed: constructed
plaintiffs: those accused
reformed: he means 'informed'
enjoin me to: impose on me
possess: tell
ought: anything
epitaph: a piece of writing in memory of the dead

BORACHIO: Yea, and paid me richly for the practice of it.
DON PEDRO: He is composed and **framed** of treachery:
  And fled he is upon this villany.
CLAUDIO: Sweet Hero, now thy image doth appear
  In the rare semblance that I loved it first.
DOGBERRY: Come, bring away the **plaintiffs**; by this
  time our sexton hath **reformed** Signior Leonato of the
  matter. And, masters, do not forget to specify, when time
  and place shall serve, that I am an ass.
VERGES: Here, here comes master Signior Leonato, and
  the Sexton too.

Re-enter LEONATO *and* ANTONIO *with the Sexton.*
LEONATO: Which is the villain? Let me see his eyes,
  That, when I note another man like him,
  I may avoid him. Which of these is he?
BORACHIO: If you would know your wronger, look on me.
LEONATO: Art thou the slave that with thy breath hast kill'd
  Mine innocent child?
BORACHIO: Yea, even I alone.
LEONATO: No, not so, villain; thou beliest thyself –
  Here stand a pair of honourable men,
  A third is fled, that had a hand in it.
  I thank you, Princes, for my daughter's death;
  Record it with your high and worthy deeds.
  'Twas bravely done, if you bethink you of it.
CLAUDIO: I know not how to pray your patience,
  Yet I must speak. Choose your revenge yourself;
  Impose me to what penance your invention
  Can lay upon my sin; yet sinn'd I not
  But in mistaking.
DON PEDRO: By my soul, nor I;
  And yet, to satisfy this good old man,
  I would bend under any heavy weight
  That he'll **enjoin me to**.
LEONATO: I cannot bid you bid my daughter live,
  That were impossible; but, I pray you both,
  Possess the people in Messina here
  How innocent she died; and if your love
  Can labour **ought** in sad invention,
  Hang her an **epitaph** upon her tomb
  And sing it to her bones, sing it tonight.
  Tomorrow morning come you to my house;
  And since you could not be my son-in-law,
  Be yet my nephew. My brother hath a daughter,
  Almost the copy of my child that's dead,
  And she alone is heir to both of us.
  Give her the right you should have given her cousin,
  And so dies my revenge.
CLAUDIO: O noble sir,
  Your over-kindness doth wring tears from me!
  I do embrace your offer, and dispose
  For henceforth of poor Claudio.

LEONATO: Tomorrow then I will expect your coming;
Tonight I take my leave. This <u>naughty</u> man
Shall face to face be brought to Margaret,
Who I believe was <u>pack'd in</u> all this wrong,
Hired to it by your brother.
BORACHIO: No, by my soul, she was not,
Nor knew not what she did when she spoke to me,
But always hath been just and virtuous
In any thing that I do know by her.
DOGBERRY: Moreover, sir, which indeed is not <u>under
white and black</u>, this plaintiff here, the offender, did
call me ass; I beseech you, let it be remembered in his
punishment. And also, the watch heard them talk of one
Deformed; they say he wears a key in his ear and a lock
hanging by it, and borrows money in God's name, the
which he hath used so long and never paid that now
men grow hard-hearted and will lend nothing for God's
sake. Pray you, examine him upon that point.
LEONATO: I thank thee for thy care and honest pains.
DOGBERRY: Your worship speaks like a most thankful
and reverend youth, and I praise God for you.
LEONATO: There's for thy pains.
DOGBERRY: God save the foundation!
LEONATO: Go, I discharge thee of thy prisoner, and I
thank thee.
DOGBERRY: I leave an <u>arrant</u> knave with your worship;
which I beseech your worship to correct yourself, for
the example of others. God keep your worship! I wish
your worship well; God restore you to health! I humbly
give you leave to depart; and if a merry meeting may be
wished, God <u>prohibit</u> it! Come, neighbour.
*Exeunt **DOGBERRY** and **VERGES**.*

LEONATO: Until tomorrow morning, lords, farewell.
ANTONIO: Farewell, my lords; we look for you tomorrow.
DON PEDRO: We will not fail.
CLAUDIO: Tonight I'll mourn with Hero.
LEONATO: (*to the Watch*) Bring you these fellows on.
We'll talk with Margaret,
How her acquaintance grew with this lewd fellow.
Exeunt, severally.

*SCENE 2. **LEONATO**'s garden.*

*Enter **BENEDICK** and **MARGARET** meeting.*
BENEDICK: Pray thee, sweet Mistress Margaret, deserve
well at my hands by helping me to the speech of
Beatrice.
MARGARET: Will you then write me a <u>sonnet</u> in praise
of my beauty?
BENEDICK: In so high a style, Margaret, that no man living
shall come over it; for, in most <u>comely</u> truth, thou
deservest it.

Dogberry confirms Don John's villainy and bad character. He lists crimes such as taking the Lord's name in vain and not paying back debts.

This is Dogberry's final speech in the play. He is as wordy as ever and reinforces the play's theme of misunderstanding – other characters do not find his words easy to follow and he misinterprets the meaning of language.

Margaret seems very relaxed and jokes with Benedick. We must presume that Leonato has already managed to speak with her and has ensured that she was innocent of meaning harm to her mistress, Hero. He mentioned his plan to do this right at the end of the last scene.

<u>naughty:</u> this would have been a stronger word than it is now, i.e. wicked
<u>pack'd in:</u> involved in
<u>under white and black:</u> confirmed in writing
<u>arrant:</u> complete, absolute
<u>prohibit:</u> he means 'allow'
<u>sonnet:</u> a fourteen-line formal poem, often with love as the subject
<u>comely:</u> attractive

Benedick wants help with writing a poem in praise of Beatrice. He and Margaret joke with each other, often using sexual innuendoes. This lightens the tone after the previous scene and prepares for the happy ending of the play.

Benedick tries to be a traditional courtly lover by writing a poem to his love, Beatrice, but he finds it impossible to find effective rhyming words.

Benedick realises he must woo Beatrice in his own way, not in the fashionable, romantic way. This could show that he is very sincere in his feelings for Beatrice.

Benedick is keen to get on to the subject of love, but first Beatrice must be satisfied that he is dealing effectively with Claudio.

bucklers: shields
Leander and **Troilus:** faithful lovers from classical tales
panders: go-betweens in arranging sexual relationships
quondam carpet-mongers: men from the past who enjoyed the company of women
in festival terms: in language of celebration
noisome: disgusting
subscribe: write down, confirm

MARGARET: To have no man come over me! Why, shall I always keep below stairs?
BENEDICK: Thy wit is as quick as the greyhound's mouth; it catches.
MARGARET: And yours as blunt as the fencer's foils, which hit, but hurt not.
BENEDICK: A most manly wit, Margaret; it will not hurt a woman. And so, I pray thee, call Beatrice; I give thee the **bucklers**.
MARGARET: Give us the swords; we have bucklers of our own.
BENEDICK: If you use them, Margaret, you must put in the pikes with a vice; and they are dangerous weapons for maids.
MARGARET: Well, I will call Beatrice to you, who I think hath legs.
BENEDICK: And therefore will come.
Exit MARGARET.
Sings
  The god of love,
  That sits above,
  And knows me, and knows me,
  How pitiful I deserve –
I mean in singing; but in loving, **Leander** the good swimmer, **Troilus** the first employer of **panders**, and a whole bookful of these **quondam carpet-mongers**, whose names yet run smoothly in the even road of a blank verse, why, they were never so truly turned over and over as my poor self in love. Marry, I cannot show it in rhyme; I have tried: I can find out no rhyme to 'lady' but 'baby' – an innocent rhyme; for 'scorn', 'horn' – a hard rhyme; for, 'school', 'fool' – a babbling rhyme; very ominous endings. No, I was not born under a rhyming planet, nor I cannot woo **in festival terms**.

Enter BEATRICE.
  Sweet Beatrice, wouldst thou come when I called thee?
BEATRICE: Yea, signior, and depart when you bid me.
BENEDICK: O, stay but till then!
BEATRICE: 'Then' is spoken; fare you well now. And yet, ere I go, let me go with that I came, which is, with knowing what hath passed between you and Claudio.
BENEDICK: Only foul words; and thereupon I will kiss thee.
BEATRICE: Foul words is but foul wind, and foul wind is but foul breath, and foul breath is **noisome**; therefore I will depart unkissed.
BENEDICK: Thou hast frighted the word out of his right sense, so forcible is thy wit. But I must tell thee plainly, Claudio undergoes my challenge; and either I must shortly hear from him, or I will **subscribe** him a coward. And, I pray thee now, tell me for which of my bad parts didst thou first fall in love with me?

BEATRICE: For them all together; which maintained so <u>politic</u> a state of evil that they will not admit any good part to intermingle with them. But for which of my good parts did you first suffer love for me?

BENEDICK: Suffer love! A good <u>epithet</u>! I do suffer love indeed, for I love thee against my will.

BEATRICE: In spite of your heart, I think; alas, poor heart! If you spite it for my sake, I will spite it for yours; for I will never love that which my friend hates.

BENEDICK: Thou and I are too wise to woo peaceably.

BEATRICE: It appears not in this confession; there's not one wise man among twenty that will praise himself.

BENEDICK: An old, an old instance, Beatrice, that lived in the time of good neighbours. If a man do not erect in this age his own tomb ere he dies, he shall live no longer in monument than the bell rings and the widow weeps.

BEATRICE: And how long is that, think you?

BENEDICK: Question - why, an hour in clamour and a quarter in <u>rheum</u>. Therefore is it most expedient for the wise, if <u>**Don Worm**</u>, his conscience, find no impediment to the contrary, to be the trumpet of his own virtues, as I am to myself. So much for praising myself, who, I myself will bear witness, is praiseworthy. And now tell me, how doth your cousin?

BEATRICE: Very ill.

BENEDICK: And how do you?

BEATRICE: Very ill too.

BENEDICK: Serve God, love me and mend. There will I leave you too, for here comes one in haste.

Enter **URSULA.**

URSULA: Madam, you must come to your uncle. Yonder's <u>old coil</u> at home; it is proved my Lady Hero hath been falsely accused, the Prince and Claudio mightily abused, and Don John is the author of all, who is fled and gone. Will you come presently?

BEATRICE: Will you go hear this news, signior?

BENEDICK: I will live in thy heart, die in thy lap, and be buried in thy eyes; and moreover I will go with thee to thy uncle's.

Exeunt.

Beatrice and Benedick enjoy good-natured teasing and joking. This is so much part of their natural behaviour, that it inevitably continues as their relationship develops. They provide a strong contrast to the other pair of lovers, Claudio and Hero, in the way they act with each other.

This is a quick way to draw the scene to an end while making sure that the main characters know what is going on. Nothing is explained to them in detail, because the audience knows all the facts already.

SCENE 3. A church; night. Claudio and Don Pedro go formally to Hero's tomb, as requested by Leonato, accompanied by torchbearers and musicians. Claudio reads out the epitaph he has written in remembrance of Hero and promises to repeat this ceremony every year.

<u>politic</u>: well-governed
<u>epithet</u>: a descriptive phrase
<u>rheum</u>: tears
<u>**Don Worm:**</u> because your conscience was thought to gnaw away inside you, like a worm
<u>old coil</u>: great trouble

Everything is now set to lead to a happy ending, with the loose ends being gradually tied up. The masked ladies continue the theme of disguise and remind us of the masked ball in Act 1 which took place before any of the problems started.

Here Benedick asks the Friar to marry him to Beatrice. Leonato now thinks that the plan to bring the couple together has fully worked.

Benedick does not understand Leonato (who is referring to the plot to bring Beatrice and Benedick together). Leonato does not go on to explain himself, because it would all get too complicated.

Don Pedro wonders why Benedick looks angry and gloomy, and this certainly seems a little strange since Benedick is in love, has just arranged to get married and is pleased that he no longer has to fight Claudio. Perhaps it is just a way for his friends to get into conversation with him, after the awkwardness of their previous meeting. Claudio jokes that Benedick is thinking about the problems that come with marriage.

- **confirm'd countenance:** serious face
- **enigmatical:** puzzling
- **conjoin'd:** joined together
- **Ethiope:** he means strange or unattractive; this seems very racist to us now, but Ethiopians would have been rarely seen, and therefore little understood by Elizabethans

70

SCENE 4. A room in LEONATO's *house.*

Enter LEONATO, ANTONIO, BENEDICK, BEATRICE, MARGARET, URSULA, FRIAR FRANCIS *and* HERO.

FRIAR FRANCIS: Did I not tell you she was innocent?

LEONATO: So are the Prince and Claudio, who accused her
Upon the error that you heard debated;
But Margaret was in some fault for this,
Although against her will, as it appears
In the true course of all the question.

ANTONIO: Well, I am glad that all things sort so well.

BENEDICK: And so am I, being else by faith enforced
To call young Claudio to a reckoning for it.

LEONATO: Well, daughter, and you gentlewomen all,
Withdraw into a chamber by yourselves,
And when I send for you, come hither mask'd.

Exeunt Ladies.

The Prince and Claudio promised by this hour
To visit me. You know your office, brother;
You must be father to your brother's daughter
And give her to young Claudio.

ANTONIO: Which I will do with **confirm'd countenance**.

BENEDICK: Friar, I must entreat your pains, I think.

FRIAR FRANCIS: To do what, signior?

BENEDICK: To bind me, or undo me – one of them.
Signior Leonato, truth it is, good signior,
Your niece regards me with an eye of favour.

LEONATO: That eye my daughter lent her: 'tis most true.

BENEDICK: And I do with an eye of love requite her.

LEONATO: The sight whereof I think you had from me,
From Claudio and the Prince; but what's your will?

BENEDICK: Your answer, sir, is **enigmatical**;
But, for my will, my will is your good will
May stand with ours, this day to be **conjoin'd**
In the state of honourable marriage –
In which, good Friar, I shall desire your help.

LEONATO: My heart is with your liking.

FRIAR FRANCIS: And my help.
Here comes the Prince and Claudio.

Enter DON PEDRO *and* CLAUDIO *and two or three others.*

DON PEDRO: Good morrow to this fair assembly.

LEONATO: Good morrow, Prince; good morrow, Claudio:
We here attend you. Are you yet determined
Today to marry with my brother's daughter?

CLAUDIO: I'll hold my mind, were she an **Ethiope**.

LEONATO: Call her forth, brother; here's the Friar ready.

Exit ANTONIO.

DON PEDRO: Good morrow, Benedick. Why, what's the matter,
That you have such a February face,
So full of frost, of storm and cloudiness?

CLAUDIO: I think he thinks upon the savage bull.
Tush, fear not, man; we'll tip thy horns with gold
And all **Europa** shall rejoice at thee,
As once Europa did at lusty Jove,
When he would play the noble beast in love.
BENEDICK: Bull Jove, sir, had an amiable low;
And some such strange bull leap'd your father's cow,
And got a calf in that same noble feat
Much like to you, for you have just his bleat.
CLAUDIO: For this I owe you: here comes other
reckonings.

Re-enter ANTONIO, with the Ladies masked.
Which is the lady I must **seize upon**?
ANTONIO: This same is she, and I do give you her.
CLAUDIO: Why, then she's mine. Sweet, let me see your
face.
LEONATO: No, that you shall not, till you take her hand
Before this Friar and swear to marry her.
CLAUDIO: Give me your hand; before this holy Friar,
I am your husband, if you like of me.
HERO: (*unmasking*) And when I lived, I was your other
wife,
And when you loved, you were my other husband.
CLAUDIO: Another Hero!
HERO: Nothing certainer;
One Hero died **defiled**, but I do live,
And surely as I live, I am a maid.
DON PEDRO: The former Hero! Hero that is dead!
LEONATO: She died, my lord, but whiles her **slander**
lived.
FRIAR FRANCIS: All this amazement can I qualify,
When after that the holy rites are ended,
I'll tell you largely of fair Hero's death.
Meantime let wonder seem familiar,
And to the chapel let us presently.
BENEDICK: **Soft and fair**, Friar. Which is Beatrice?
BEATRICE: (*unmasking*) I answer to that name. What is
your will?
BENEDICK: Do not you love me?
BEATRICE: Why, no; no more than reason.
BENEDICK: Why, then your uncle and the Prince and
Claudio
Have been deceived; they swore you did.
BEATRICE: Do not you love me?
BENEDICK: Troth, no; no more than reason.
BEATRICE: Why, then my cousin Margaret and Ursula
Are much deceived; for they did swear you did.
BENEDICK: They swore that you were almost sick for me.
BEATRICE: They swore that you were well-nigh dead for
me.
BENEDICK: 'Tis no such matter. Then you do not love me?
BEATRICE: No, truly, but in **friendly recompense**.

Claudio has yet another test to pass before he deserves Hero: he is not allowed to look at the face of his bride until he has promised to marry her.

This is a dramatic moment. Although the audience knows that it is Hero behind the mask, there is interest in how Claudio reacts and how the lovers behave towards each other. Hero forgives Claudio absolutely, holding no resentment about what has happened.

As usual, Beatrice and Benedick say far more to each other than Claudio and Hero do. At last they realise how they have been tricked by their friends into confessing their love. It almost seems as though nothing will come of it, when Beatrice says she just loves Benedick as a friend, but Claudio and Hero come to the rescue by revealing the sonnets the pair have written to each other.

Europa: a girl from Greek mythology; Europa was carried off by the god Zeus, who had taken the shape of a bull
seize upon: take (in marriage)
defiled: with her reputation damaged
slander: a false and damaging spoken statement about someone
soft and fair: Benedick wants the Friar to pause a moment, to give him a chance to talk to Beatrice about marriage
friendly recompense: as a friend

Even in her last speech in the play, when she agrees to marry Benedick, Beatrice carries on with her teasing manner. For once Benedick manages to make her be quiet, by kissing her!

No teasing can destroy Benedick's good mood or his intention to marry. He admits that he has not behaved consistently, but declares that this is human nature. He also re-establishes his friendship with Claudio, who will now be related to him by marriage.

It is Benedick who dominates the end of the play. Apart from saying the most, he directs the action. He wants dancing before the marriages and overrules the more senior Leonato, who thinks the dancing should come afterwards. Look at the ending of the Kenneth Branagh film to see how joyfully this section has been presented.

The final loose end is tied up when we hear that Don John has been captured, but this news is not allowed to dampen the happy atmosphere.

LEONATO: Come, cousin, I am sure you love the gentleman.

CLAUDIO: And I'll be sworn upon't that he loves her;
For here's a paper written in his hand,
A **halting** sonnet of his own pure brain,
Fashion'd to Beatrice.

HERO: And here's another
Writ in my cousin's hand, stolen from her pocket,
Containing her affection unto Benedick.

BENEDICK: A miracle! Here's our own hands against our hearts. Come, I will have thee; but, by this light, I take thee for pity.

BEATRICE: I would not deny you; but, by this good day, I yield upon great persuasion; and partly to save your life, for I was told you were in a **consumption**.

BENEDICK: Peace! I will stop your mouth.

Kissing her.

DON PEDRO: How dost thou, Benedick, the married man?

BENEDICK: I'll tell thee what, Prince; a college of wit-crackers cannot flout me out of my humour. Dost thou think I care for a satire or an **epigram**? No; if a man will be beaten with brains, 'a shall wear nothing handsome about him. In brief, since I do purpose to marry, I will think nothing to any purpose that the world can say against it; and therefore never flout at me for what I have said against it; for man is a giddy thing, and this is my conclusion. For thy part, Claudio, I did think to have beaten thee; but in that thou art like to be my kinsman, live unbruised and love my cousin.

CLAUDIO: I had well hoped thou wouldst have denied Beatrice, that I might have **cudgelled** thee out of thy single life, to make thee a double-dealer; which, out of question, thou wilt be, if my cousin do not look exceedingly **narrowly** to thee.

BENEDICK: Come, come, we are friends. Let's have a dance ere we are married, that we may lighten our own hearts and our wives' heels.

LEONATO: We'll have dancing afterward.

BENEDICK: First, of my word; therefore play, music. Prince, thou art sad; get thee a wife, get thee a wife. There is no staff more reverend than one tipped with horn.

Enter a MESSENGER.

MESSENGER: My lord, your brother John is **ta'en in flight**,
And brought with armed men back to Messina.

BENEDICK: Think not on him till to-morrow; I'll devise thee brave punishments for him. Strike up, pipers.

Dance. Exeunt.

---

halting: not flowing well
fashion'd: constructed
consumption: pining away
epigram: a short, witty poem
cudgelled: beaten
narrowly: closely
ta'en in flight: caught while escaping

ACT 5 QUESTIONS

Understanding the plot
1. Who is Leonato prepared to fight?
2. Who is Claudio meant to marry instead of Hero?
3. How frequently does Claudio intend to visit Hero's tomb?
4. Why does Claudio not at first realise that his bride is Hero?
5. What news is there of Don John?

Who says this?
1. 'My soul doth tell me Hero is belied.'
2. 'You are a villain – I jest not'
3. 'Choose your revenge yourself.'
4. 'The former Hero! Hero that is dead!'
5. 'Come, I will have thee, but by this light I take thee for pity.'

Name the character
1. Who refuses to accept good advice?
2. Who tries to write a poem to express his love?
3. Who writes an Epitaph to put on Hero's tomb?
4. Who is going to be married at the end of the play?
5. Who tells Don Pedro that he should find himself a wife?

Understanding character
1. What is the attitude of Don Pedro and Claudio, when they are talking to Benedick about Leonato's and Antonio's challenge to them: disrespectful/fearful/angry?
2. Why does Benedick not joke with his friends?
3. How does Claudio react when he realises he has wronged Hero?
4. How does Claudio react when he realises Hero is alive?
5. How do Benedick and Beatrice contrast with Claudio and Hero just before their marriage?

Themes and imagery
1. Fighting: Who says his wit is now in his scabbard (a sheath for a sword)?
2. 'Don Worm' is an expression Benedick uses to describe who or what?
3. Disguise: In what way is this theme returned to in the last scene?
4. What does Don Pedro mean when he says that Benedick has 'such a February face'?
5. Love/marriage: What effect on the mood does the music and the dancing have at the end of the play?

73

Empathy tasks

Writing in role means writing as if you were one of the characters. You may have to do this in the form of a letter or a diary or simply a stream of consciousness. For example, you may be asked to pretend that you are Beatrice, writing a diary after she has fallen in love with Benedick, explaining her sudden change of heart.

A checklist for empathy tasks

● Try and imagine what that character might be thinking or feeling.

● Always use evidence from the play as the basis of your ideas.

● Focus on the set scenes, but refer to the play as a whole.

● Make sure you write in a convincing way – in other words, don't make it too modern. Don't say 'I was gutted by what Benedick said', instead say 'I was heart-sore at Benedick's words'.

● Try and use some of Shakespeare's language, e.g. 'I did think Benedick was nothing but the Prince's jester and a very dull fool, but now I know differently'.

Write in role (empathy) questions

Question styles

In your SATs exam you will be asked to answer a specific type of question. There are three main types of question.

Analyse presentation of theme or character

Pretend to be the director

Directing scenes

You may be asked how you would direct the two scenes you have been studying. Specifically, you could be asked to focus your response on the advice you might give one or two characters, or you could be asked how you would present the whole action in terms of atmosphere, mood and effects.

A checklist for director tasks

● Imagine how the scenes would look if they were performed on stage.

● Think about how the characters' feelings can be shown by the way they say their lines.

● Try and consider stage directions and take these into account.

● Use evidence from the text to justify your views, e.g. 'Hero is described as "modest", so she needs to look shy during this scene, perhaps with her eyes looking at the floor as if she is nervous'.

● Always base your advice on what you know is happening in the play.

● Always think about the effect you want to have on the audience.

Analytical questions

For these questions you will be expected to show your understanding of the way that the language choices affect mood, atmosphere, characterisation, themes and the action. You must be able to compare two scenes, commenting on:

● Development of character
● Vocabulary choices
● Imagery
● Sound effects
● The change between verse, prose or songs.

A checklist for analytical tasks

To obtain maximum marks in these questions, always remember:

POINT → EVIDENCE → EXPLAIN

74

PLANNING AND STRUCTURE

STEP 1: THE QUESTION

The first thing to do is to READ THE QUESTION. Then re-read it, to make sure that you know *exactly* what you are being asked to do. Next, highlight key words. This will help you focus on what is really wanted. You must also re-read the printed extracts, thinking about, and perhaps highlighting, which parts will be relevant to your answer. *If bullet points are provided you should pay attention to all the suggestions in them.*

STEP 2: PLAN YOUR RESPONSE

Now comes the PLANNING. An organised approach to your answers is very important if you want to impress the examiner and to SHOW YOUR UNDERSTANDING of the play. You are far less likely to run out of things to say if you have made some sort of plan to guide you. How you plan really depends on what works best for you. Here are some ideas:

● A list of points – perhaps numbered according to paragraphs

● A spidergram or other diagram with key words and quotations

● Annotations around the set scene.

STEP 3: GETTING STARTED

You can now START YOUR ESSAY. It is important to start confidently, making a clear point in the first sentence, so that the examiner thinks, 'Here is a candidate who is in control and knows what they're talking about'. If you start well, you will also feel better about the task, which should be reflected in your performance.

STEP 4: POINT, EXAMPLE, EXPLAIN

As you write your response, remember the formula:
POINT → EXAMPLE → EXPLAIN.
The idea is that you make a point, back it up with a quotation and then say a little bit more to show that you have really thought about what you are saying:

> point
>
> Benedick is convinced that Beatrice is in love with him, for he imagines that he can 'spy some marks of love in her'. This is a complete contrast to his attitude in the first Act and the word 'spy' suggests he is examining her every move.
>
> explanation
>
> example/quotation

Notice that a short quotation has been used. This is effective and blends smoothly into the sentence. Sometimes you will want to include a whole line or two, but never quote long passages. You haven't got the time and it isn't necessary.

STEP 5: TAKE CARE

Throughout your answer be organised and remember to use paragraphs. TAKE CARE with spelling, punctuation and expression so that the examiner can follow your work easily.

STEP 6: AND FINALLY ...

Remember to leave time to draw your answer to a strong, clear CONCLUSION. You could sum up your main point or give your personal opinions in the final paragraph. Leave a few minutes to check through your writing carefully. Good luck!

MODEL ESSAYS

Act 1, Scene 3 and Act 2, Scene 2

Imagine that you are Don John in these two scenes. Write down your thoughts and feelings after hearing about Claudio's marriage plans.

EXAMINER'S TOP TIP

This is an <u>empathy task</u>, so make sure you write in a <u>suitable tone of voice</u> for Don John, using clues from the text. Remember he is <u>miserable, likes to cause trouble</u> and does not get on very well with his brother. He is also jealous and <u>does not like his brother's friends</u>, so he would be very <u>unhappy about the news</u> of Claudio's marriage.

PARAGRAPH 1

- Begin by setting the scene and putting the action in context:

  'I thought things were bad enough when I had to make peace with my so-called brother, but now I am even more annoyed.'

- You are an illegitimate brother and you are not respected by your brother or by society.

- Explain how you are feeling after fighting your brother, giving some details about the fighting (use your imagination).

Act 2, Scene 3 and Act 3, Scene 1

In these scenes Beatrice and Benedick overhear information about each other. As a director, what advice would you give to the actors playing these roles?

EXAMINER'S TOP TIP

This is a <u>director-style question</u>, so you must remember to look closely at how Shakespeare uses <u>stagecraft, language and character interaction to entertain the audience.</u> You must also <u>compare the two scenes</u> and show that you understand how the advice you give the main characters will be different for each scene.

PARAGRAPH 1

- Discuss the staging of Act 2, Scene 3 and briefly explain what happens.

- Consider how you would like Benedick to speak his long prose speech about Claudio:

  'Benedick must sound very forceful here when he talks about the effects of love. He is allowing the audience into his personal thoughts, and if he seems passionate about the negative effects of love it will make his transformation at the end of the scene more contrasting. At the end he should almost spit the words "Monsieur Love" to show how much he hates the thought of being in love.'

Act 1, Scene 1 and Act 5, Scene 2

These scenes feature Benedick and Beatrice. How has their relationship developed over the course of the play?

EXAMINER'S TOP TIP

This is an <u>analytical-style question</u>, so you must remember to look closely at how Shakespeare uses <u>language and imagery to develop characters.</u> You must also <u>compare the two scenes</u> and show that you understand how Beatrice and Benedick have changed and how the <u>audience can see this development</u>. Remember, always use:

POINT→EVIDENCE→EXPLAIN.

PARAGRAPH 1

- Discuss the characters of Beatrice and Benedick at the start of the play, explaining that they are two of the main characters and that they both dominate the action at the start.

- Explain Beatrice's character in Act 1, Scene 1 – she is strong, witty and does not want to get married.

- Briefly talk about Benedick's character – he is intelligent, a good soldier but also funny and against marriage.

PARAGRAPH 2

- Explain why you do not like any of Don Pedro's friends. (You could mention how Claudio has taken what you see as your place by being friends with Don Pedro).
- Talk about the conversation you had with your friend Conrade when you told him about your feelings (you could include some quotes.)

'I explained everything to Conrade and he seemed to understand. He knows that feeling this way fits my blood. I don't care what people think because I am happy being a plain-dealing villain.'

PARAGRAPH 3

- Talk about how you heard about Claudio's marriage from Borachio and give details about Don Pedro's plan to woo Hero for Claudio.
- Comment on how you regard Hero and Claudio.

'I hear Claudio is to marry Hero, Leonato's daughter. It would be a good match for him. He is a **very forward March-chick** to go after her so quickly. He's barely a man. I can't see what she sees in him.'

PARAGRAPH 4

- Now you can talk about Borachio's great plan to upset the wedding plans.

'Luckily, Borachio has thought up a brilliant scheme to ruin things.'

- Say how pleased you are to be able to ruin things and that you don't mind paying Borachio lots of money for his part in the plan.
- You could end by thinking about the future and other ways you could cause trouble.

PARAGRAPH 2

- Discuss the staging of Act 3, Scene 1 – you could mention that in contrast to the other scene, this one begins without Beatrice on stage. The audience knows what is happening by listening to Hero.
- Explain how you would like Beatrice to look when she comes on stage to eavesdrop:

'Shakespeare has Hero refer to Beatrice as a "lapwing" who "runs close to the ground". Therefore, the actress needs to scuttle on stage as quickly as she can, looking eager to hear the conversation, but also, perhaps, a bit guilty.'

PARAGRAPH 3

- This paragraph needs to concentrate on how Benedick reacts when overhearing his friends.
- Choose phrases from the scene and discuss his changing reaction. For example, during Balthasar's song he must still take an anti-romance stance, so he might sneer at the words, but later when he hears phrases like **'she will die'** he could look amazed and delighted.
- Look carefully at the stage directions, and indicate where you want Benedick to talk to himself, as well as where the other characters need to talk straight at the audience.

PARAGRAPH 4

- Now you can look closely at the remainder of Act 3, Scene 1, in the same way that you looked at the other scene.
- Think carefully about how Beatrice would react when she hears herself being described as someone who 'cannot love'. Would she agree and nod to herself, or would she look outraged?
- Now give advice to both characters after their friends have disappeared:

'Benedick has a brief meeting with Beatrice and must look as if he is examining her every move and word. He should look smitten, so Beatrice would probably give him strange looks. Beatrice, however, stands alone on stage and delivers a soliloquy directly to the audience, filled with questions, "Can this be true?". She should look a bit puzzled.'

PARAGRAPH 2

- Discuss how Benedick and Beatrice interact in Act 1, Scene 1.
- These characters share many qualities and their arguments are not hurtful, but a form of witty banter and teasing.
- Beatrice may say she does not like Benedick but she can not stop talking about him when he is not around.
- Discuss the images they use about each other: **'Lady Disdain'**, **'court jester'**.

PARAGRAPH 3

- This needs to be a short paragraph explaining how Beatrice and Benedick realised that they were perfect for each other.
- Be careful not to simply re-tell the story, but show you understand the play as a whole.

PARAGRAPH 4

- Now you can look closely at the language in Act 5, Scene 2.
- Refer to Benedick's actions on stage – he sings because he is so happy and tries to make up a love poem for Beatrice.
- Benedick compares himself to other famous lovers, such as Troilus and Leander.
- Discuss how the characters talk to each other and explain how Benedick has challenged Claudio to a duel to prove his love.

77

SATS EXAMINATION QUESTIONS

1 Act 1, Scene 1 and Act 2, Scene 3
Compare the behaviour of Benedick in these two scenes and comment on the changes that you notice in the way he acts and speaks.
- What strong impressions do you get of Benedick's views and manner in the first scene?
- Examine his views on love.
- Look at his interactions with his male friends and with Beatrice.

2 Act 2, Scene 3 and Act 3, Scene 1
In these scenes Beatrice and Benedick overhear information about each other. As a director, what advice would you give to the actors playing these roles?
- How would the characters react when they are listening to their friends talking?
- How would they say their aside comments?
- How would they behave once their friends, on whom they have been eavesdropping, have left the scene?

3 Act 1, Scene 1 and Act 5, Scene 2
These scenes feature Benedick and Beatrice. How has their relationship developed over the course of the play?
- What are their changing attitudes to love and marriage?
- What has brought about a change in the relationship?
- Remember to quote to illustrate how they speak to and about each other.

4 Act 1, Scene 3 and Act 2, Scene 2
Imagine that you are Don John in these two scenes. Write down your thoughts and feelings about Claudio's marriage.
- What is your opinion of Claudio, your brother's closest companion?
- Why are his marriage plans of any interest to you?
- What would be a suitable tone/mood for your thoughts, to bring out your character?

5 Act 2, Scene 1 and Act 3, Scene 3
How is the idea of deception developed in these two scenes?
- What kinds of deception are taking place?
- What are the motives for being deceptive?
- Is the mood comic or serious in these scenes?

6 Act 2, Scene 3 and Act 4, Scene 1
These two scenes show how being in love affects people. Write about the ways Shakespeare demonstrates that falling in love can make characters behave in different ways, using ideas from the play.
- Which characters are involved in the love plots in these scenes?
- What examples of extreme behaviour do you notice?
- Do these characters behave differently now that they have fallen in love?

7 Act 4, Scene 1 and Act 5, Scene 4
Imagine that you are Claudio. Write a letter to the Friar, after you have married Hero, thanking him for his involvement and explaining how you felt when you thought Hero had been unfaithful and why you acted in the way that you did.
- What mood would you be in as you write this letter?
- Has Don Pedro influenced how you acted?
- What hopes do you have for the future?

8 Act 1, Scene 1 and Act 1, Scene 3
These scenes feature the brothers Don Pedro (Act 1 Scene 1) and Don John (both scenes). Compare the ways that these characters are portrayed and the ways that other characters interact with them.
- What are your first impressions of each character?
- What do they think of each other?
- How does their use of language differ?

9 Act 1, Scene 2 and Act 5, Scene 1
Look closely at the presentation of Leonato and Antonio and comment on how both men behave in these scenes. Do we see different sides of their characters at these different stages in the play?
- Remember what the relationship is between these two characters.
- Do both men show the same attitude to events?
- How do other characters react to them?

10 Act 3, Scene 3 and Act 4, Scene 2
These scenes feature Dogberry and Verges. As a director, what advice would you give to the actors playing these roles?
- How would you get the humour across?
- Would they have particular accents or mannerisms?
- How would the characters react to each other?

78

ANSWERS TO END OF ACT QUESTIONS

Act 1

Understanding the plot
1 Don Pedro, Benedick, Claudio and company
2 He is now on good terms with his brother, Don Pedro.
3 Benedick
4 Don Pedro will woo her on his behalf at the masked dance.
5 Conrade and Borachio

Who says this?
1 Beatrice   4 Don Pedro
2 Benedick   5 Claudio
3 Don John

Name the character
1 Claudio   4 Benedick
2 Don John   5 Borachio
3 Antonio

Understanding character
1 Benedick
2 He has fought very well in the wars for such a young soldier.
3 Benedick
4 He is confident that Don Pedro will do the best for him and succeed in arranging the marriage, and he cannot really refuse an offer made by the Prince.
5 He sees Claudio as having all the honour, position and attention that should really be his.

Themes and imagery
1 Don John
2 Hero and Claudio
3 Beatrice and Benedick
4 Benedick's
5 Claudio (by Don John)

Act 2

Understanding the plot
1 A combination of Don John and Benedick, because one is silent while the other talks too much
2 She has too sharp a tongue.
3 She describes him as a court jester, always playing the fool.
4 In Leonato's orchard
5 The information comes from Hero, and Leonato is old, wise and can be trusted.

Who says this?
1 Beatrice   4 Benedick
2 Beatrice   5 Claudio
3 Don John

Name the character
1 Don Pedro   4 Margaret
2 Benedick   5 Beatrice
3 Don John

Understanding character
1 He never says anything and is always miserable.
2 Claudio, when he thinks Don Pedro has wooed Hero
3 Benedick
4 She says he is far too grand for someone like her.
5 Borachio, Don John's companion

Themes and imagery
1 It offers lots of opportunity for confusion, humour and mistaken identity.
2 Nice clothes, sweet music and fine words
3 Benedick, after Beatrice offends him
4 That he is always centre of attention, has lots of stories and likes making people laugh
5 It was a place where you wept after losing your loved one.

Act 3

Understanding the plot
1 Hero, Ursula and Margaret
2 By talking about his great reputation across the country
3 Because she has been having an affair with Borachio
4 One thousand ducats
5 Borachio and Conrade

Who says this?
1 Hero   4 Benedick
2 Ursula   5 Don Pedro
3 Beatrice

Name the character
1 Margaret   4 Benedick
2 Don John   5 Leonato
3 Dogberry

Understanding character
1 Hero uses reverse psychology and claims that Beatrice would never love Benedick.
2 He pretends to be very upset by the information.
3 They provide comic relief and make the audience laugh when things get too serious.
4 He anticipates that there might be trouble at the wedding the next day.
5 He immediately believes Don John without talking to his fiancée.

Themes and imagery
1 Beatrice overhears the ladies gossiping and Don John spreads lies about Hero.
2 Beatrice
3 Having toothache
4 This Latin cure, meaning a medicine made from thistles, is a sly reference to Benedick, who is making Beatrice love-sick.
5 Her sadness is a premonition of Claudio's intentions the following day.

Act 4

Understanding the plot
1 He believes that Hero is not a virgin and has met a man in her room on the night before the wedding.
2 He will be told that she has died as a result of the accusation against her.
3 She will go to a religious institution – probably a nunnery.
4 Borachio
5 He has fled from Messina.

Who says this?
1 Claudio   4 Beatrice
2 Leonato   5 Dogberry
3 Benedick

Name the character
1 Leonato
2 Don Pedro and Don John
3 Friar Francis
4 Dogberry and Verges
5 The Sexton

Understanding character
1 The serious side
2 She is innocent and therefore totally shocked by what he says and how he behaves.
3 They are honourable men, so he cannot believe that they would lie.
4 Benedick
5 Self-important

Themes and imagery
1 Hero
2 Beatrice and Benedick
3 Hero
4 Hero looking innocent, but being false (according to Claudio); the pretence that Hero has died, so there will be an appearance of mourning
5 Claudio

Act 5

Understanding the plot
1 Claudio
2 Antonio's daughter
3 Once every year
4 She is wearing a mask.
5 He has been captured.

Who says this?
1 Leonato   4 Don Pedro
2 Benedick   5 Benedick
3 Claudio

Name the character
1 Leonato
2 Benedick
3 Claudio
4 Claudio and Hero; Benedick and Beatrice
5 Benedick

Understanding character
1 Disrespectful
2 He is angry with them for the dishonourable way in which they have behaved.
3 He is deeply sorry and distressed and is happy that Leonato should take his revenge. He will also do anything that Leonato wishes.
4 Claudio is stunned but delighted. He says 'Another Hero!' but nothing else for some time.
5 They still joke with one another; they have a far more informal relationship and know each other much better.

Themes and imagery
1 Benedick
2 Conscience (Scene 2)
3 The ladies are in masks when Claudio comes in to claim his bride.
4 Benedick looks cross and disapproving.
5 It makes the mood light-hearted and full of harmony – appropriate for a happy ending.

INDEX